The Map or the Territory
Notes on Imperialism, Solidarity, and Latin America in the New Millennium

by
Clifton Ross

New Earth Publications
Berkeley, California

New Earth Publications
Copyright © 2014 Clifton Ross

Direct inquiries to:
Clifton Ross
P.O. Box 2642
Berkeley, CA 94710

ISBN 13: 978-0-915117-57-4
Front cover photo and design
by Clifton Ross
Back cover photo by Scott Braley

Printed in the United States of America.

The Map
or
the Territory

Introduction

A map can be a very useful guide to a territory, unless the territory has so dramatically changed that, at some point, it bears little, if any, resemblance to the map. I doubt very much that I'd be able to find my way around Berkeley, California, the town I live in, using a map from 1848. Even an up-to-date street map of my city will do very little to help get me around town if I'm driving a car: the map doesn't indicate the traffic barricades throughout the city which make it almost impossible to get across town on side streets.

Maps can also distort real geography in ways that give us a false idea of relative proportions, which can translate into a distorted view of reality in many respects. This is particularly true of the Mercator map, created in 1569 to serve the Europeans who were sailing southward to Africa as slave traders, and westward across the Atlantic to expand their empires. Despite having been debunked for its inaccuracy, the Mercator projection is still manufactured and commonly used in the United States.[1]

Because the Mercator map is drawn from the perspective of the Europeans, who first used it, the equator is found 2/3rds of the way down the map, making the countries of the Northern Hemisphere appear larger than those of the Southern Hemisphere. What impact would this representation have on European or North American students of geography, or average citizens who grew up with this vision of the world?

Perhaps an exaggerated sense of national size, and therefore, power and importance. On the other hand, what impact would this distortion have on South Americans or Africans, many of whom have also grown up seeing that image on the walls of their classrooms? Maps are created by and for geopolitical powers; territories are where people live and interact with one another and their environment. Maps can be deeply ideological tools for social formation and control, making it necessary, in some cases, to reject them in favor of the specific territories we know to exist.

Ideology, too, is a type of map, delineating reality and routing passages from one idea to another like roads from city to city, connecting seemingly independent centers and giving rational order to what would be a mere jumble of groups with no connections to each other. Like a map, ideology indicates theoretical boundaries, assigning to ideas and groups varying degrees of importance, some greater and others lesser, according to the perspective of its originators. And while ideology can orient and offer direction and coherence to a complex intellectual geography, it can also distort and falsify.

I will argue in this book that this is precisely the situation in which many of us on the left find ourselves today. The ideologies of the 19th century are in many ways as irrelevant to our current situation as a hundred and fifty-year-old map of my hometown. While some of the general features (streams, hills and valleys) may remain the same, others may have undergone dramatic changes. In the pages that follow, I will argue that it's time that we update our ideologies by assessing their relevance to current realities, by comparing our maps to our territories, as it were.

7

I began writing the pages that follow between different legs of a national tour that my wife Marcy Rein and I undertook in 2014 to promote our book, *Until the Rulers Obey: Voices from Latin American Social Movements* (Oakland: PM Press, 2014). Everywhere we went we met with the same questions, so I began thinking about writing a book to try to summarize some of the research, experiences and rethinking I'd been doing as Marcy and I put our book together.

It's not an exaggeration to say that the process of working on *Until the Rulers Obey (UTRO)* changed my life. Over the period of seven or so years, from the time of its conception to its publication, I can now see I was in the process of a slow transformation that reached its denouement in the final months leading up to the completion. That story is worth recounting here as it will enable the reader to understand the angle I've taken in this present work which is, I think it's fair to say, distinct from much of the left's view of Venezuela, especially here in the United States.

The process that ended with the publication of *UTRO* really began in 2003 when Marcy and I went to Oaxaca, Mexico to celebrate my having finished work on my Masters degree, graduating at the age of fifty from San Francisco State University. It had been a difficult transition for me to make, leaving my life as a printer, writer and activist with a focus on Latin American revolutionary movements to spend nearly three years removed from life in the environment of academia, studying to become an English teacher.

After obtaining my degree, I needed to return to Latin America to see if I could, through such a journey, find a way of reconnecting with that part of myself I'd lost touch with while immersed in academic work. I felt nostalgia for my "second language personality" that had begun to emerge in Spanish twenty years before when I'd lived and worked in Nicaragua during the romantic and painful years of the Sandinista Revolution. I sensed, somehow, that I might find that lost persona on this journey and integrate it into my life in the North.

We flew to Mexico City and caught a bus to Oaxaca where we spent time interviewing teachers gathered in the yearly *plantón* (occupation) in the city's plaza. Marcy was working at the time at the International Longshore and Warehouse Union (ILWU), and the struggle of teachers in Oaxaca was captivating and inspiring for both of us, even if we saw it from slightly different angles. From Oaxaca we went on to Juchitán, in the Isthmus of Tehuantepec, to meet with one of the teachers we'd gotten to know at the plantón, and then on to Chiapas where we visited the Zapatista community of Oventic.

Returning to San Cristóbal we caught another bus to Comitán near the Guatemalan border to meet people in the Popular Education Collective of Comitán and see what we could learn from them about popular education in Mexico. The main force behind the collective was clearly Antonio, a man a few years older than I who was already suffering the debilitating effects of Parkinson's disease. Despite his frailty, he was a brilliant and inspiring man with a passion for the work of the collective, which he articulated with great poetic power.

We were fascinated to hear of their work in the communities of Chiapas, doing education and conscientization with a focus on the Puebla-

9

Panama Plan. But what moved me most was something Antonio mentioned proudly, if incidentally. The collective, he told us, had a near complete collection of the papers from the Sandinista Ministry of Education which were moved out of Nicaragua when the Sandinistas lost the elections in 1990. Fearing that the files would meet the same fate as the textbooks and many other important documents from the Sandinista Revolution that the UNO government of Violeta Chamorro was burning in hopes of eliminating any trace of that decade of history, the Minister of Education, Fr. Fernando Cardenal and others in the Ministry had managed to get the papers safely to Mexico where they were now safe-housed in Comitán.

I realized then that some strange twists of fate had led me along this tortuous road to Comitán to reencounter my own spiritual path, but there it was. I didn't need to see the papers. I just needed to remember that I had a path, and that it led through Nicaragua.

I returned north, and taught my first year of ESL at Berkeley City College. Then the following summer I returned to Nicaragua to see if I could find some of the old Sandinistas who had "kept the faith" and not fallen victim to the temptation that the "Piñata" represented; that disgraceful moment, after the electoral defeat of the Sandinistas and before the new government assumed power, marked a second moral defeat of the Revolution.

There may have been some justification for the process of dividing up the country's wealth, given that the Sandinistas had led the process of "reconstruction" after the revolutionary struggle that had removed the US-backed dictator Anastasio Somoza from power in 1979. They must have rationalized that after all, they hadn't managed to provide themselves with any security for the future during the years of Revolution, and now they'd be leaving office with nothing, and certainly without prospects for the future, as revolutionaries in what they knew would become a neoliberal outpost under Chamorro's rule.

They no doubt further rationalized that dividing up the wealth of the country would be a way to "protect it for the people" when they eventually did return to power. Overnight the *comandantes* of the Revolution became the wealthiest people in the country, especially Daniel Ortega and his brother Humberto, but Jaime Wheelock, Tomas Borge and others also came out immensely wealthy.

The "Piñata" was the beginning of the end of the Revolution, or at least the Revolution many of us in the United States had come to love and support. And there had been thousands of us—tens of thousands—who had visited the country over the decade during which the Sandinistas had been in power.

There were Christians like me (at the time) who had seen in the Sandinista Revolution "the breaking forth of the Kingdom of God," the most beatific expression of Liberation Theology. The Sandinista Revolution was certainly Liberation Theology's high water mark. There were also Marxists, progressives of all stripes, liberals, and just good people who felt it was wrong that Ronald Reagan was sending terrorists to attack a country equivalent in size, population, economy and military strength to the state of Alabama. Along with the Sanctuary movement, solidarity with the struggles of Central America brought more people

11

out into the streets than any other movement, with the exception of the Anti-nuclear movement.

Part of the reason was the cruelty, evil and complete unjustifiability of what came to be known as the "Contra War" that caused everyone aware of it intense emotional outrage. In every branch of government, the US political system demonstrated once again in those years its moral depravity and cynicism as it sent Nicaraguan mercenaries, trained by Argentine officers fresh from their own country's Dirty War, to murder and terrorize the Nicaraguan civilian population.

But some of us also learned a little more about ourselves during that decade of guerrilla struggle in Central America and solidarity organizing at home, especially about our limitations. We weren't able to stop the attacks, although Witness for Peace did a brave and noble job of protecting lives with their own bodies in the war zones, and many dedicated souls, Nicaraguans and internationalists from all over the world including the US, threw themselves entirely into the work of defending the Sandinista Revolution.

I'd been part of the Christian left, living a few years in an Anabaptist community, before joining Christians for Socialism. As those associations ended I worked on my own as a translator and editor. I produced pamphlets, poetry and translations of materials from Nicaragua's Christian Base communities and printed them on presses at worker collectives I was a part of or in the basement of collective houses in Berkeley where I lived. I learned a lot from that experience, and as so often happens, I learned most through pain and failure.

I remember a particularly poignant moment, some time in June of 1987 when I was briefly living in Managua. I'd taken the afternoon off from the Guatemalan news agency where I was working and rode my little Yamaha 175 to the market to do some shopping. It was the usual scene, like being in the jungle and listening to and watching all the bright birds sing and preen and flit about, and I was one of them. It was a beautiful hot day in Managua so the shade of the market stalls offered a cool respite from the afternoon sun as I wandered, called to by the market ladies to buy from them. As usual, I had very little money so I just continued walking gradually toward the section where I hoped to buy some dried beans. Suddenly the voices around me stopped and all eyes turned toward two Sandinista policemen making their way through the market.

I felt a jolt of confusion. Here were the representatives of the state with which I was working in solidarity, policemen "of the people" who in earlier years had been celebrated and loved. Yet now the people in the market had fallen into a sudden hostile silence at their appearance. In that instant I recognized some contradiction I couldn't quite process. I therefore tried to put the incident out of mind, as I went on to make my purchase and ride down the Panamerican highway home.

I managed if not to forget that moment, at least to shrug it off. I told myself it had no meaning, but it remained as a sharp, painful image, one that would return to me two and a half or so years later, the day after the Nicaraguan elections of February 1990.

KPFA radio in Berkeley was covering them and everyone was expecting the Sandinistas to win another great victory. The polls, even those of the "bourgeois" press, had forecast as much, and Larry

Bensky was on hand to do up-to-the-minute reporting—from Nicaragua—if I'm not mistaken. But as the returns came in, it became clear that the Sandinistas had lost. For me it was devastating. Like many others, I felt, of all things, betrayed. The Nicaraguans had let us down! We'd put so much of *our* faith, *our* time, *our* energy into defending *their* Revolution: how could they do this to *us*?

I admit to feeling some shame even now as I write this, but I need to be honest. What I realized was that this was the first real moment of complete honesty I'd had in my years of solidarity work. Like most partisans, I'd been honest about the real gains of the revolution's "process," but not about its potential problems. When I was living in, or visiting, Nicaragua, I hadn't been honest about the graffiti I'd tried to ignore that said, "Alto a la burocracia Sandinista" (End the Sandinista Bureaucracy); the theft that had grown among the formerly "revolutionary" Sandinista policemen, who, like everyone else in the country living through the hell of an out-of-control economy, had grown desperate and taken measures to protect themselves any way they could; and I hadn't been honest about that day in the market, or what it could have told me about where things *really* stood in the country, not where I imagined, or conceived them to be based on the ideological frame that I'd imposed on reality.

The pain was intense. I was like a man who has seen himself all his life in the face of his hero to be reasonably handsome and attractive, pleasant and appealing, only to pass a mirror and in an instant see his real disfigured visage. I, the revolutionary who looked to the beautiful Che, the divine Jesus, as my models, now saw myself in the

14

image of the hunchback of Notre Dame or the Phantom of the Opera.

The reaction, I now see, was exaggerated, but it was an exaggerated reaction to an exaggeration. I had worshipped these men and held such high ideals for them and for myself that my simple, mortal failure seemed worthy of hell or eternal exile. And I was ashamed of those fallen idols. They had proclaimed the highest of ideals, but in their failure, didn't display any of the shame that I felt.

The experience—exaggeration and all— served its purpose, leading me to swear never to perpetuate such dishonesty by first denying to myself what I was seeing, and then enabling a cascade of lies, instead of doing the real work of critical solidarity.

This was a turning point in my life that coincided with other changes, forming part of a process of real transformation from idealistic, and perhaps also ideological, political commitments, toward a more integrated commitment to myself, my community and my world. Now I see how that also initiated an ongoing process of recovery from dishonesty of many kinds. People who live in extreme states often project an idealized self to hide their powerful shadow. This was clearly as true for the Sandinistas who had engaged in the Piñata as it had been for me, personally.

So now, some fourteen years later, I was ready to head to Nicaragua for the summer to interview Fernando and Ernesto Cardenal. My dear friend David Fetcho gave me a crash course on using a video camera, and I left. I returned to the old neighborhood of Bolonia, nicknamed "Gringolandia" for the number of internationalists who frequented the hospedajes (guest houses) in the Sandinista years. I spent most of the summer there, and passed the twenty-fifth anniversary of the Sandinista Revolution in Managua, although I didn't have the heart to go to the Sandinista celebrations.

I went to meet Ernesto Cardenal at his House of Three Worlds cultural center where we'd arranged to do an interview. It was in the middle of that interview that I suddenly realized what my next move needed to be. I had asked him what he thought of President Lula, but he wasn't interested in discussing him. Instead, he said, "Venezuela under Chávez, now that's something else." He spoke enthusiastically of the Bolivarian Revolution and encouraged me to visit there.

So, on Cardenal's advice, six months later I spent most of Christmas vacation in Venezuela. I met Franz Lee and his wife Jutta Schmidt, and a number of Chavistas in Mérida, and within a short time I'd caught the excitement. I went home determined to spend more time in Venezuela, and returned in June to spend the summer. While there, I accepted an invitation to participate in the Second World Poetry Festival of Venezuela and spent a week meeting poets from all over the country and the world. I traveled a bit around the country with my video camera and recorded interviews, which I later edited into a feature-length film.[2] I lived for nine months in Mérida, elated to be back in Latin America. In March 2006 I fulfilled a life-long dream to travel through the Southern Cone and up through Peru where, at last, I visited Machu Picchu.

I returned home after a yearlong absence in June 2006 but then during every break I had from teaching, I went back to Venezuela, always landing first in Mérida where I stayed with my friends—my

16

second family—Humberto Martinez and Betty Osorio at the Teatro Colibrí (Hummingbird Theater).

In early 2008 my movie came out, and later that year another writer and I decided to work on a book of interviews with social movement activists throughout Latin America, lending my lust for travel a purpose. I spent 2009-10 gathering interviews in a number of countries for what would eventually become *Until the Rulers Obey* but didn't return to Venezuela until 2011.

Despite my absence during that time, it was becoming clear to me, even from a distance that serious problems were starting to erode the Bolivarian process, but at that point I wasn't ready to focus on them, even if I did acknowledge them, as Chavistas did, in a general way. The corruption and self-enrichment that marked the elite Bolivarian clique in power earned them the nickname "Boliburgos" (Bolibourgeois), which I found increasingly disturbing, especially given the impunity that accompanied it.

By 2012 the other writer had dropped out of the book project and left it to Marcy and me to complete. We decided to take a trip to Chile, Argentina and Uruguay to do some final interviews. While in Uruguay we set up a time to meet with Raul Zibechi and one morning at his house, talked with him at length about the problems confronting the social movements in Latin America. In response to my question about what he saw as the major problem confronting the ones under the progressive governments of the "Pink Tide," he responded, "the major problem they face is the progressive governments." The Pink Tide governments' ability to coopt the movements with money extracted from mining and other industries going on under their watch was unprecedented in recent years.

Marcy and I returned to the US and wrote the introduction to our book and then I began digging deeper. Surely Zibechi's critique wouldn't apply to Venezuela, I thought. But the more I dug, the more apparent it was to me that what I had been seeing over the previous eight years in Venezuela was not as I thought it was. I continued to do more research as I revised and rewrote, and again revised and rewrote, my introduction to the Venezuela section of our book. And just as I was finishing what I thought was my final draft on March 5, 2013, the phone rang. It was a friend calling to tell me that Chávez had died.

I knew then I had to return to Venezuela to see if my research jibed with what I saw on the ground there, so I left, filled with many questions on a trip to Venezuela, which I timed to coincide with the elections of April 2013.

It would require too much space even to summarize my experiences in Guayana, the industrial heartland of Venezuela, in Mérida and Caracas, interviewing workers and members of the left opposition, and of the opposition in general, but by the time I left the country a month later, my views had completely changed about what I understood to be happening in Venezuela under the Bolivarian government. [3] The beating of members of the opposition in Parliament, a coordinated attack by PSUVistas, with Diosdado Cabello looking on, wasn't the most shocking incident, but it certainly was emblematic of the violent turn the PSUV was taking, especially when its hold on power was threatened. [4]

I returned home that May 2013 in the painful beginnings of a transformation resulting from a new understanding I'd gained from many meetings with people in the left opposition like Margarita Lopez Maya, Damian Prat (whose excellent book, *Guayana: El Milagro al Reves* had a powerful impact on me), Rafael Uzcategui (anarchist editor of *El Libertario* and author of *Venezuela: Revolution as Spectacle*) and the union workers in the Basic Industries of Guayana. The late Emilio Campos, Secretary General of the union, Sindicato de Trabajadores de CVG *Carbonorca* (Sutracarbonorca) who died tragically in a car accident a little over a year later (in June 2014), made a special impression on me for his passion and his commitment.

I began studying and reading people I'd heretofore ignored, such as Javier Corrales and Michael Penfold whose *Dragon in the Tropics*, presented a very different, and very credible narrative on the Venezuelan process. I began studying the populist tradition in Latin America and following the economic news and fitting what I was learning into the emerging picture.

The Map or the Territory is a work-in-progress and a current synthesis of where I understand the processes in Latin America to be and where I see them .going from here. I'm convinced that the "Pink Tide" is receding and the radical projects will begin to moderate or collapse. I try to offer an explanation here of why I believe that to be happening and what our response should be as a left that looks to Latin America for inspiration and hope.

I attempt to offer here a look at Latin America in general, and Venezuela in particular, "from below," that is, from a social movement perspective. I emphasize the article "a" since social movements and their members have a diversity of perspectives, a fact which gives them their particular dynamism. I make the assumption that the reader is sympathetic to the processes for social transformation underway in Latin America so I've concentrated on a critical analysis of the negative dimensions of the problem for the most part, given that my ideal reader is already fairly familiar with some of the positive changes in the region.

I make no specific forecasts about what changes might take place in the region in the future, but I do try to indicate what I see as general trends already occurring, with a focus on Venezuela. No doubt history will prove me wrong in at least a few particulars, but I hope my honesty and good will are evident in these pages, and that the work as a whole will help educate people and open up much-needed dialogues on the left that so far have taken place only in academic circles.

Clifton Ross
Berkeley, California
September 2014

Acknowledgements

Thanks to my old friend Michael Duffy who gave much encouragement to me on an earlier draft. Thanks to B. Jesse Clarke who also offered several very good "political directions" as I wrote this book. Thanks also to Kevin Rath, whose company and conversation many Saturday mornings have helped me clarify much of the problematic I've considered in these pages. Special thanks to Elizabeth Claman who helped edit this manuscript and improved it greatly. All errors are, of course, my own.

The first and last acknowledgement is to Marcy, my co-editor and partner in life, love and struggle. Her clarity in challenging my ideas and beliefs continues to inspire me to strive ever harder in my search for truth.

Part One:
Notes on Imperialism, Solidarity and
Latin America in the New Millennium

A Note about Money, Words, Signs and Symbols

Seeing then that truth consisteth in the right ordering of names in our affirmations, a man that seeketh precise truth had need to remember what every name he uses stands for, and to place it accordingly, or else he will find himself entangled in words, as a bird in lime twigs—the more he struggles, the more belimed... By this it appears how necessary it is for any man that aspires to true knowledge to examine the definitions of former authors; and either to correct them, where they are negligently set down, or to make them himself. For the errors of definitions multiply themselves according as the reckoning proceeds, and lead men into absurdities which at last they see, but cannot avoid without reckoning anew from the beginning, in which lies the foundation of their errors.
Thomas Hobbes, *Leviathan*

In some parts of the world, birdlime is still used to catch birds. It's a sticky substance, the composition of which varies from place to place, but if it's put on the twigs of a tree, when a bird lands, it finds itself unable to fly away. As Hobbes notes, the more the bird struggles, the more it is "belimed" and unable to fly.

Language should liberate, but in our time, especially in the realm of politics, it becomes a snare. This is no accident, as demagogues transform the words and ideas that should be welcome resting places so that like "belimed" birds, we are trapped and struggle against forces we only dimly recognize. Other such tangles are of our own making and still others are part of the natural process of language as things and processes evolve beyond the original symbols which then no longer accurately reflects them.

To remedy the situation of our entanglement in a web of words and ideas, we might take Hobbes' suggestion to heart: He says if we wish to have "true knowledge" we must return to the original definitions, or else redefine words and ideas anew for ourselves because "the errors of definitions multiply themselves according as the reckoning proceeds, and lead men into absurdities" unless they make the necessary corrections. Once the correction is made, progress in the desired direction can again become possible. Where the correction is not made, one is doomed to remain in the "tangle" of old or erroneous ideas that don't correspond to the real world.

A great number of the problems of political language, however, are indeed the result of demagogues and Madison Avenue executives intent on manipulating "voters" or "consumers" trapped in their spheres of power. It's no accident if that evokes images of dollar bills, as there are reasons beyond the obvious ones for that connection. To a great degree, the problem with political discussions in the US, and increasingly across the planet, is that currencies around the world have been debased. Let me explain by way of a minor digression.

Originally, money was a form of exchange used in bartering. It was made of electrum, a fusion of silver and gold. By means of its use, Rome had a lively market society, but eventually its expenses exceeded its supply of money. Then that old goat Nero came up with a solution: He began putting out smaller coins with his image on them, immediately increasing the supply, and also giving birth to that curious phenomenon known as "inflation." Other governments were even craftier, mixing in baser metals than gold or silver, which "debased" the currency. Markets, and those who operated in them, particularly the merchants, quickly caught on to this ruse and charged more for their products to gain the same value (or more) than what they'd gained before.[5]

Fast-forward to the twentieth century and the remarkable moment of Bretton Woods when the US dollar went off the gold standard and began to represent itself. Overnight the paper that became the world's currency had no reference to anything other than itself. From this fact surged what some have called the "Post-Modern Condition": Symbols no longer represented anything but themselves *as symbols*. David Hawkes writes, "Until the early twentieth century, it was officially declared and popularly believed that all the money in the world could theoretically be converted into gold. Money was a sign, but it had an ultimate, material referent. In postmodernity, however, money has become an autonomous, self-generating, inconvertible sign—a signifier with no signified."[6]

It might seem far-fetched to correlation money with our thought processes, but the two are actually closer than we might want to believe. Especially in a consumer society. As Georg Simmel points out, "The idea that life is essentially based on intellect, and that intellect is accepted in practical life as the most valuable of our mental energies, goes hand in hand with the growth of a money economy."[7]

How this relates to political discussions (and most ideological ones, be they religious, philosophical or other) is that increasingly, the symbols have supplanted anything concrete, so rather than referring to objective realities, they increasingly express only subjective identities or meanings.

As this pattern continues to perpetuate itself, a new world system is emerging, dreadful and seductive, but a largely fictional construction, and one, I would argue, constructed to contain and control the majority. If we hope to alter the course this system has set for us, we have leave behind the tangle of worn-out ideas and return to original meanings, questioning our basic assumptions about the world. If we don't, if we grow complacent, in a very short time we might slip into extinction. But, if we're diligent in our work to unmask this construction, we might open a door to a world we never dared dream possible.

And those are precisely the stakes at present: transformation of ourselves and the world system, or death. Solidarity with people and their struggles in other lands might have been seen as "optional" in the past; now it has become an absolute necessity for the people of the world to unite to stop the destruction of the earth and its life. While governments and their representatives have spoken of the need to stop climate change, they have done very little to stop the slow-moving catastrophe. Now, more than ever, it's clear that change will only happen if people take the lead, and force the governments into submission to the laws of life.

Just as people the world over see the need and feel the desire to transform the world economic system known as "capitalism," powerful governments are equally united in maintaining its continuation. The present world system is defined by globalized capitalism where "transnational capitalists and allied dominant strata integrate horizontally and in the process move 'up' cross-nationally, penetrating and utilizing numerous national and transnational state apparatuses to forge their rule," William Robinson argues. And he adds, "...a counter-hegemonic project led by popular classes would need to do the same."[8]

If we look into our past for a "counter-hegemonic project" that would "integrate horizontally and in the process move 'up' cross-nationally," I would argue that we need look no further than the internationalist solidarity movements of the anti-capitalist, anti-imperialist left. That is our "beginning" point, to which we must return, as it were, untangling one twig at a time until we are free from the tangle in which many of us presently find ourselves: struggling to break free of old ideas that no longer work so we can begin to define new ones that will illuminate directions into the future.

26

Empire from the Inside Out

The United States of America was the bastard creation of an apparent contradiction: an anti-colonial struggle with aspirations to become an empire. This bastard child, not surprisingly, would grow up to develop a schizoid personality: one side of which was sociopathic, amoral and filled with the most insatiable greed; the other side would hunger in its isolation for community, to unite with all humanity, guided by the high ideals of the Republic in their most radical meaning. Each of these personalities would in time give birth to movements that would descend to our own day: the culture of empire, and its contrary, the counter-culture.

No sooner had it broken free of Great Britain in the first revolution of the modern era than the newly formed nation of the United States of America began building its own empire from within. The colonization of native lands was part and parcel of a racist genocide in which slaves were also brought in from Africa to work the newly conquered lands, still red with the blood of their former occupants. Not surprisingly, the first anti-imperialists were forced to work close to home in their struggle for justice, humanity and a democratic republic so severely threatened by the emerging empire.

And so the first anti-imperialist struggles in the United States can be traced back to the birth of the nation from the blood and fire of the "Indian Wars" that accompanied westward expansion, and the Abolitionist movement that sought to end the "peculiar institution" of slavery. The history of this early struggle is rich, complex and inspiring but we'll only sketch the barest outline of this movement since its history is vividly recounted elsewhere.[9]

There were two major strands that came together in the Abolitionist movement. On one side were the religious and spiritual figures, the Quakers, Evangelicals and those swept up by the Great Awakening of Methodism, among others. These included Harriet Beecher Stowe, John Woolman and many whose opposition to slavery and to the genocide against Native Americans (for the two went hand in hand in the expansion and building of the American Empire) was rooted in their religious faith and values.

A second strand was represented by James Oglethorpe, Thomas Paine and others influenced by the Enlightenment. Their opposition was rational and consistent with the anti-colonial, anti-imperialist ethos that inspired the American Revolution in the first place. The first anti-slavery society formed in 1775 in Philadelphia in the midst of the revolutionary struggle, and Thomas Paine was among its founders.

The internal expansion of the American empire and the imperialist hunger for more territory led to war with Mexico in 1846, cheered on by the great majority of North Americans. A small minority, nevertheless, articulated a stance that would inspire generations. Henry David Thoreau's civil disobedience was individualistic, extreme and principled, and wholly in keeping with the abolitionists and the forces struggling against the Indian Wars.

Naturally, the most consistent, committed, and militant in the struggle against the internal imperialist expansion and colonialism were the victims of this process themselves. Here Frederick Douglas stands out for his clarity, commitment and courage, calling the Mexican-American War "a slaveholding crusade." The Native Americans, as well, fought bravely against all odds through the end of the 19th century and beyond. They, along with the African-Americans—both the slaves of the past and descendants of slaves today—continue that struggle. The list of well-known Native Americans to have given their lives in the struggle against the empire is long; the list of those anonymous warriors is infinite. To their ranks have now been added the other peoples all over the globe, plundered and tyrannized by the Empire and now living within it: those of Pilipino, Chinese, Vietnamese, Korean, and Latin American descent.

The Anti-Imperialist League

In 1898 the American Anti-Imperialist League was formed as an unlikely coalition, which included the likes of industrialist Andrew Carnegie and labor leader Samuel Gompers, along with workers, retired bankers, religious figures and humanitarians, all upset over the Spanish American War and the US invasion and occupation of the Philippines. Mark Twain soon joined in and became one of the most articulate voices of the movement, along with Edgar Lee Masters, Ambrose Bierce, William and Henry James and others.

It's true that "The anti-imperialist movement was really an upper class white movement" (and even male dominated) and some of its "members had grave doubts whether or not the United States could absorb other races into its system" believing that by "adding the Philippine problem to the mix...the Constitution could collapse." But to qualify all the members of the League as "conservative" and somehow racist is unfair: It was far too diverse in the opinions of its members to be portrayed with such broad strokes.[10] Despite all its shortcomings and historical limitations the Anti-Imperialist League still "represents a high-watermark of anti-imperialism in the United States."[11]

In fact, regardless of their race and class origins, the American Anti-Imperialist League in their pamphlets and other writings more than anything expressed moral outrage and indignation over the violation of the principles of the republic. Far from celebrating the racism underlying the imperial venture undertaken in the Philippines, the writers denounced it and called for the "capable" people of that nation to choose their own destiny, free from the violence visited upon them by the US government and its troops.[12] The platform of the League appealed to liberal democratic principles on which the North American republic was founded:

> We hold that the policy known as imperialism is hostile to liberty and tends toward militarism, an evil from which it has been our glory to be free. We regret that it has become necessary in the land of Washington and Lincoln *to* reaffirm that all men, of whatever race or color, are entitled to life, liberty and the pursuit of happiness. We maintain that governments derive their just powers from the consent of the governed. We insist that the subjugation of any people is "criminal aggression" and open disloyalty to the distinctive principles of our Government.[13]

The League rejected the "ancient heresy that might makes right." They regretted the shedding of Pilipino blood and expressed horror over the "the "betrayal of American institutions at home." Referring to the recent Civil War, which had taken place in their own lifetimes and contrasting it with the 1898 US invasion of the Philippines, they said, "The attempt of 1861 was to divide the country. That of 1899 is to destroy its fundamental principles and noblest ideals." The League promised to oppose for reelection any official supporting the disgraceful wars against the Philippines, Puerto Rico and Cuba, and ended with a quote from Lincoln: "Those who deny freedom to others deserve it not for themselves, and under a just God cannot long retain it."[14]

The membership of the League dwindled away and was finally disbanded in 1921 but it witnessed to the moral conviction and valor of a significant part of the population and to the US intelligentsia at a crucial moment in the nation's history. Sadly, their voices were drowned out by cheers for the imperialist Progressives organized around Theodore Roosevelt, whose "Rough Riders" became a symbol for the rising American empire.

The Communists Arrive

The next big wave of solidarity activism arose in the wake of the Russian Revolution and was in great part sponsored by the Comintern (International Communist Party), which saw the struggle against imperialism as simply an extension of the worldwide struggle against capitalism. There were certainly other actors in the movements against the United States' attempts to expand its empire beyond the continental borders. African-Americans, for instance, organized to fight for Haiti in "their own independent anti-imperialist organizations – such as the Negro National Anti-Imperialist and Anti-Trust League and the Colored National Anti-Imperialist League." [15] African-American soldiers from the US had also been known to defect from the US army and switch over to fight with the Pilipinos, just as African-Americans had done with Native Americans in previous decades.

The Socialist Party of the USA was another major force for solidarity, particularly with the Mexican Liberal Party, founded by, among others, the anarchist Magón brothers. Members like John Turner were also well known for their defense of Mexican migrants and workers in the United States. The Socialist Party integrated a broad array of the left wing of Populism, the anarchist and syndicalist left and democratic socialists that emerged in the 19th century, but in that sense it was the party of the past even at its founding in 1901.

While its decline was gradual, the Socialist Party was destined to eventually give way to the more energetic Communist Party of the USA (CPUSA) born in the midst of the repression of 1919. After all, the CPUSA enjoyed prestige by association with the first successful "socialist" revolution in the history of the world in Russia, and its big tent for radicals eventually drew even the likes of members of the anarcho-syndicalist union, the Industrial Workers of the World like "Big Bill" Haywood and anarchists like Emma Goldman.

Under the liberal Democrat Woodrow Wilson the attack against the left was fierce. The criminalization of speech, with the 1917 Espionage Act and the Sedition act of 1918, were the initial steps toward the nation's first "Red Scare" that led to the Palmer Raids and to repression, exile or imprisonment, physical attacks, and a barrage of propaganda against the US left. This campaign of terror under Wilson's government effectively wiped out significant parts of the independent left, such as the anarchists, social democrats, and socialists. Only the Communists and the Socialist Party of the United States emerged from that war on the left relatively intact, even continuing to grow and build membership.

Over time, the influence of the Communist Party on left politics in general, and on the anti-imperialist movement in particular, became more pronounced. The All-America Anti-Imperialist League, which founded the "Hands-Off Nicaragua Committee" in Mexico City to gain solidarity with Nicaraguan patriot Augusto Sandino's struggle, was "a front founded in 1925 by the Third Communist International (Comintern)." [16] Despite Sandino's choice of colors, which indicated his anarcho-syndicalist beliefs, the support he received, brief as it was, came primarily from the Communist movement.

But the CPUSA had complicated relations with Moscow and, while it played a leading role in anti-imperialist and anti-colonial struggles in the

US until World War II, its power declined due to its support of Stalin and the show trials in the Soviet Union. Then its influence further withered under the assault of the second Red Scare under Joseph McCarthy.

Despite the decline of Communist standing, the CPUSA held a hegemonic influence on the US left, if for no other reason than its association with a powerful world-wide anti-capitalist organization based in the home of the world's first communist revolution. Over time, the CPUSA was forced into deeper cover and its policy of building a united front with other leftists and liberals suffered greatly. On the other hand, it seemed to be blindsided by emerging left struggles that chose the path of armed insurrection over the political struggle.

Solidarity with Guerrilla Struggles
1959-1989

Throughout the 20th century the Comintern's relations with the guerrilla movements of Latin America were complex and full of conflicts. For the most part it viewed armed insurrection as "adventurist" and not in keeping with its policy of building a united front with local bourgeoisies around the world. Like the Socialists, the Communists held a "'stageist' view of history – a conception of progress in which all societies must move through certain discrete stages of economic development, or modes of production."[17]

Guerrilla-led insurgencies didn't square with the official policy of the Comintern in "underdeveloped" countries, which was to support the bourgeoisie in building capitalism so that eventually, the economy in question could become transformed, first into state capitalism, and then communism, through stages.

Fidel Castro only received support from the Soviet Union reluctantly after he won power in 1959 in a protracted guerrilla war. Much of Castro's moral support initially came from liberal democrats and others disgusted by the Batista dictatorship against which Castro and his rebels fought. In fact, it could be argued that Castro was initially more enthusiastically received by liberals in the US than by his eventual communist allies.

The US government, obsessed as it was in those years to hunt down communists and persecute them, spent surprisingly little time—only a week, in fact—deliberating over whether or not to recognize the Castro regime, despite its having come to power through armed insurrection. Notwithstanding some suspicions about his political views and those of the leftists, like Ernesto "Che" Guevara, who had fought with him, the US allowed Castro's visit four months later, during which time he toured the country and even met with then Vice-President Richard Nixon.

Nevertheless, Castro's would be the last guerrilla insurgency to which the US would be willing to give the benefit of a doubt. And as the US geared up to militarily defeat guerrilla warriors and national liberation movements, most notably in Vietnam, new solidarity movements were emerging in the US and worldwide to combat US policies.

Although the emerging solidarity movements were not simply communist front groups but rather very diverse organizations with members who held equally diverse ideologies and views, the Marxist-Leninist vanguard conception remained the dominant ideological backdrop to most of the leftist movements in the US. This was especially so in 1969 and after when the radical left, including the Trotskyist Socialist Workers Party, played an increasingly large role in anti-imperialist struggles, especially around the Vietnam War.

In a sense, many of the solidarity groups and left formations internally identified the guerrilla organizations of the country with which they were in solidarity as their own vanguard. The National Liberation Front flag of North Vietnam was frequently flown in later demonstrations (after 1969) where Ho Chi Minh's name was chanted and communiqués from the "Viet Cong" were read.[18]

There was, however, another anti-imperialist left which was very significant, and remains so to this day, even if it was overshadowed by the Marxist-Leninist left that gradually took a hegemonic role in the anti-imperialist struggles against the wars in Southeast Asia. In fact, the pacifist, religious anti-imperialist left were the first ones on the protest lines in front of the White House in the early 1960s. The Catholic Workers, members of the traditional peace churches like the Quakers and Mennonites and others quietly carried out their small vigils and were integrated in the groundswell of resistance as the war in Vietnam developed. They were the first ones on the front lines of struggle against the empire-builders who took power in the U.S. and they will, in all likelihood, be the last ones standing. Unfortunately, they remain, for the most part, the unsung heroes of that struggle, even in most histories.[19]

Nevertheless, among the later Latin American solidarity organizations, especially after the victory of the Sandinista National Liberation Front in Nicaragua, July 19, 1979, the vanguardist formation was more explicit and Fidelista communism became the underlying, even if often unacknowledged, orthodoxy.

Although Christians played a major role in the Sandinista process in Nicaragua, and in the US, their contribution was an often overlooked or embarrassing detail to many in the US solidarity movement. At times splits occurred within these organizations because one side felt the other was not adhering strictly enough to the line of the vanguard party with which the organization was in solidarity.

Even though a Leninist ideology came to dominate much of the solidarity movement, it was often cloaked with democratic language so as to appeal to a wider North American public. But the solidarity organizations' relationship to the guerrilla forces and victorious anti-colonial governments, particularly to Cuba, Nicaragua and the liberated territories of El Salvador, was consistent with Leninism. By the post-Vietnam era, the idea of a vanguard party and "democratic centralism" was so naturalized on the left that it was simply assumed that any anti-imperialist struggle should be subordinated uncritically to the will of the vanguard party with which it was in solidarity.

With the collapse of the USSR and the demise of Sandinista rule in Nicaragua, the signing of the peace accords in El Salvador in 1992 and the end, one by one, of the guerrilla insurgencies throughout Latin America, along with many Marxist parties, much of the solidarity movement disbanded. Leftists the world over began to return to "beginnings" to try to untangle themselves from failed ideas and to redefine the "left" in some new form.

Meanwhile, in Latin America

Together both the struggles that started with direct conflict against US invaders from the beginning to the middle of the 20th century, as well as the guerrilla wars against US colonial regimes in the second half of that century represented a second decolonial struggle in Latin America. It was, of course, preceded by the long struggle against Spain, extending throughout the 19th century. And both the 19th and the 20th century were characterized as "national liberation" struggles, that is, as *political* struggles for *political* independence.

But Latin Americans fighting for independence and many of their allies worldwide recognized that economic independence was arguably far more significant than political independence. Under Spain and the early years of US colonialism, Latin America's economies were based on extraction and exploitation of prime resources and raw materials, the list of which is endless: silver, gold, guano, copper, sugar, rubber, oil, minerals, plants, animals... Trade relations imposed by colonial powers and regular imperial interventions reinforced these exploitive relations and imperial policies were generally designed to ensure that Latin America would not develop manufacturing capabilities.

The Great Depression of 1929 and the devastating impact it had on Latin America convinced many regional governments to develop their own industries. Doing so, it was believed, would make them more independent and less vulnerable to international economic downturns. They recognized that the first to suffer, and the most vulnerable, in an economic recession would be those providing raw materials for the productive processes. And so from the early part of the twentieth century until the early eighties, Latin America's economic model was based on import substitution industrialization (ISI).

The ISI economic model was a state-led, state capitalist model of development often associated with the corporatist regimes of Latin America, in particular Argentina under Juan Peron, Brazil under Getulio Vargas (1930-1945) and Mexico under the Institutional Revolutionary Party. Corporatism, commonly and rightly associated with fascism, took many distinct forms in Latin America, even as it drew from the more authoritarian motherlands of Franco's Spain and Salazar's Portugal. The philosophy of corporatism, with deep roots in Roman Catholicism, was a natural fit for Catholic Latin America and it could even be viewed as a left alternative that conformed to the anti-communist line of the United States but gave workers some limited role in society. And ISI was a perfect companion economic approach since "state capitalism and ISI in the national economic life required similarly statist and authoritarian controls in the social and political spheres."[20]

The ISI development model was given further impetus by Raul Prebisch and the neo-Marxists or "structuralists" associated with him in the 1950s. His ideas were distilled in the Singer-Prebisch thesis, which indicated that inequality in terms of trade between the "periphery" and the "center" implied the fact that over time nations at the periphery would need to sell an increasing amount of raw materials in order to afford to buy the manufactured goods they needed from the industrial "center." This idea was the basis for the "dependency theory," which became popular on the left in the 1960s-1970s. It posits that the resolution to the problem of underdevelopment would be for nations at the periphery to industrialize and manufacture the products they needed themselves.

ISI was essentially a strategy on which virtually everyone could agree – corporatists, military dictators, Marxists, and even, eventually, the United States. Despite strong US opposition to ISI early on, and especially to the Marxists and those deemed "communists" who advocated the policy, eventually the empire came around. As Panitch and Gindin point out, "It is largely forgotten today that US foreign economic policy in the 1950s actually supported Import Substitution Industrialization (ISI) as a development model and that this was underwritten by the Federal Reserve's endorsement of greater national control over monetary policy in the Third World."[21]

While the Marshall Plan for Europe was US government financed, Washington decided on allowing the multinational corporations to put their hand to helping develop Latin American industry. Eventually, "a report in 1951 by the US representative to the Organization of American States indicated that American officials were 'much impressed with the work of the ECLA (UN Economic Commission on Latin America) and... especially with Dr. Prebisch [who] is in a position to bring home to Latin American officials economic truths which they would not accept on the basis of any statement made by US representatives.'"[22] From the perspective of US and international capital, ISI policies were helping transform Latin America from a "backward" natural/peasant economy into a large, modern market economy ready for investment by multinational corporations. In that sense, the US government and its capitalist

class apparently shared with the Marxists the
"stageist" view of history.

ISI and its Consequences on the People

And so it was. As Latin America began to industrialize, along came factories, and these required workers. Farmers, *campesinos*, left the countryside and their subsistence farming for jobs in the factories, becoming members of the working class. Unions arose to organize the workers and represent their demands for higher wages and better working conditions, and the ISI model appeared to be working for many as the living standards of most Latin Americans began to improve through the mid-twentieth century.

But the unions and parties representing the working class often came into direct conflict with the governments, which commonly owned the factories, and they were also (in this Cold War context) viewed as inspired by Soviet communism, which, in many cases, they were. Throughout the region, corporatist military dictatorships (especially in South America) and democratic, but right-wing governments backed by Washington, resorted to "disciplining" the workers through increasingly repressive measures which included imprisoning, terrorizing, "disappearing," torturing and murdering on a massive scale anyone deemed to be a leftist.[23] These repressive policies had a radicalizing effect, in some cases (particularly in Central America 1950s-1980s) driving many workers into the ranks of vanguard guerrilla armies where they were joined by their campesino relatives from the countryside.

The situation grew worse as Latin America raced through money trying to catch up to the "First World" in terms of development and to be able to compete with their products on the international market. Banks, awash in Arab money from the spike in oil prices due to the oil shock of 1973, began lending more and more to Latin American governments, egged on by the US government. This happened at the same time that these Latin American governments were attempting to move from ISI (wherein, as the name implies, imports were substituted with goods manufactured within the country) to exports that could compete on the international market. Governments of the region welcomed the offers of more loans as a chance to increase capitalization and thereby gain a competitive edge in the global marketplace.

By the late 1970s the ISI model, at least as it was implemented in Latin America, began to show weaknesses. The economies of the region began to sputter and fail just as Federal Reserve Chairman Paul Volker jacked up interest rates in the United States. In the words of David Harvey: "Since the loans were designated in US dollars, however, any modest, let alone precipitous, rise in US interest rates could easily push vulnerable countries into default."[24] The higher interest rates increased the debts of the Latin America governments such that soon payments on the interest alone ate up "from 33 to 59 percent of total export income between 1979 and 1981."[25]

Mexico was the first to threaten default, at which time the US sent in the good cop in the form of the IMF with a "structural adjustment program that became a model for the rest Latin America and beyond."[26] Other governments across the region followed Mexico in a wave of privatizations aimed at paying off the massive national debts. The 1980s became known in Latin America as "The Lost Decade," during which incomes across the region plummeted, the guerrilla wars in Central America intensified and the dictatorships of South America began to fall. The factories were privatized, and many closed; unions began to weaken before the overwhelming economic catastrophe of a premature deindustrialization.

And then, around the world, rumblings were heard from the impending collapse of the Union of Soviet Socialist Republics.

The New Epoch of Globalization

The collapse of the Soviet Union coincided with the globalization of capitalism. Some, like William Robinson, argue that the dramatic changes that came about in production as a result of globalization represented "an epochal shift in world capitalism."[27] In this new world, a new "transnational capitalist state"(TNS) and a new "transnational capitalist class" (TCC) would emerge to work through transnational institutions like the World Bank (WB), the World Trade Organization (WTO), the International Monetary Fund (IMF) and others, in accordance with new legal agreements like General Agreement on Tariffs and Trade (GATT), and other international agreements aimed at facilitating "free trade" and the movement of capital in its search for the cheapest labor on the planet.

How different was the shift to globalization? We'd agree with Robinson that it was nothing less than "epochal." This shift in capitalist production would come to transform the world in ways we are still attempting to understand. Many successful businesses that had one time been "national" had long since "grown up" to become "multinational corporations," but now they morphed into "transnationals." This process sounds complicated, but it's really very simple.

A Very Brief Primer on Globalization:
In Search of The Ultimate Gizmo

Imagine mom and pop with their little storefront in Centerville, USA, incorporating and going national with their gizmo. When they start out, they're just one of hundreds of thousands of small business across the country. But as they grow they first build their own factory and sell to surrounding cities, then surrounding states, and eventually they begin eating up their competitors until they outgrow even their own country in terms of productive capacity.

Eventually, they might sell their gizmo factory in Centerville because they want to bring down the cost of one of their greatest expenses, specifically labor, so they can make more money. Now that their gizmo is one of only a few others in the world, they pack the plans up and send them to a factory in China to make the gizmo for them, transforming Mom and Pop, Inc. into a "multinational corporation."

Over time, the gizmo becomes The Gizmo, at which time Mom and Pop, Inc. might move their money off to the Cayman Islands, incorporate in Panama, and have all the various parts of The Gizmo made at specialized plants in different parts of the world, shipping them to China to be assembled in the prisons or factories from whence they are sent out to the Walmarts of the world on ships flying the flag of Belize.

That's globalization. And it's no wonder that ISI and Latin America's dreams of development in this scheme are things of the past. There's simply no way that individual nations implementing ISI policies can compete with the level of competition represented by worldwide chains of production, given current conditions. Globalization has, in a sense, remapped the world of production.

On the map of global capital, the world is now divided up into specialized regions, each playing its unique part in the process of building The Gizmo. China, with its enormous population, would be the perfect assembly plant, given its cheap labor and a government willing to fiercely crack down on workers at the first signs of demands for better wages or working conditions. But it doesn't have the iron, the lithium, the oil or many other components needed to make The Gizmo. That's where Latin America comes in.

Plans like the Initiative for the Integration of the Regional Infrastructure of South America (*IIRSA*), drawn up by Brazil's last neoliberal president, Henrique Cardoza, and now apparently implemented by the region's governments, including those of the Pink Tide, indicate that Latin America will play the role of providing all the raw materials for Mom and Pop Inc.'s Gizmo. Latin America would be returned to its place in the feeder chain of digging metal out of the earth and lending its rich soils to monocultures for paper, food and energy to run the global steam shovel that rams all this material into the Chinese Gizmo factory.

The United States still played the role of Enforcer with its enormous military, and was also the one to initiate the whole process with the victory party for Capitalism in its "Cold War" against the Soviet Union, a moment hailed as the "End of History." The future was bright for Mom and Pop, Inc. and all those in their class who had made it to the top of the global capitalist food chain.

But the celebrations didn't last long.

Starting Over from Scratch

Just as the world Communist movement was throwing in the towel, a new force was already emerging. It was also very much inspired by Latin American guerrillas, but guerrillas of a very different kind. Many of those associated with what would later become known as the anti-globalization movement began to formulate their ideas in tandem with the Zapatistas.

The trademark ski masks of these South Mexican rebels spoke of their rejection of personalist politics even as their articulate and delightfully witty spokesperson, *Subcomandante* ("El Sup") Marcos rose to the fore. He was a real "personality" who captured this new generation of activists with his poetic, post-modern idiom with which he expressed an ecumenical left perspective steeped in the deep indigenous wisdom of the continent's native people. And the fact that the Zapatistas had timed their uprising with the implementation of the North American Free Trade Agreement to demonstrate that their interests surpassed mere local and parochial concerns was a fact that was not lost on remaining and emerging leftists around the world.

These qualities of the Zapatistas, especially as displayed by Marcos, appealed to the new generation of activists who were coming up from the rubble of twentieth-century communism and attempting to redefine "left" in their battle against globalized capitalism. Their anarchistic, egalitarian politics, and clarity about changes in the world capitalist system contrasted sharply with the older "New Left's" Marxist-Leninist (vanguardist) perspective.

Along with the Zapatistas, this new generation of activists refused the idea of "taking state power." Not only would such an act be unlikely, given the capitalist state's increasing technical superiority in logistics, weaponry and surveillance, but even in the unlikely case that they won power in a "post-Communist" world, they would then simply be forced into the position of administering a capitalist state directed by a globalized TCC. "Counter-power" in social movement became a form of guerrilla strategy to attack the static, stationary state power of the *status quo*.

There were many small skirmishes that served to educate youth entering the battlefield against globalizing capital, but the big battles were still to come. On the cusp of the millennium the new movement found their opportunity to take on a major symbol of the newly defined enemy, the World Trade Organization. The "Battle of Seattle" was the first major battle of an assembly of unionists, environmentalists, Zapatistas, people from all over the country and, indeed, the world, united against the WTO on November 30th 1999. The new movement shut down the international organization's meeting and locked the city of Seattle down.

The Pink Tide: Ebb and Flow

The "Pink Tide" governments of Latin America are usually associated with changes in the region at the turn of the millennium, but the first example of these moderately progressive governments was a product of a new US policy of "democracy promotion" implemented in the 1980s. The 1990 victory of the center-left coalition of political parties known as the "Concertación," coming after the 1988 referendum that removed General Augusto Pinochet from power, represented a new moment in the region.

The victory of the center-left Concertación was an indication, for the first time, that the US would be willing to tolerate "socialists" in Latin America, as long as they were willing to play by Washington's neoliberal rules. The Concertación obliged. Their reward was their ability to rule the executive branch of the Chilean government through their presidents for the next twenty years until the people, in a *"voto de castigo"*(punishment vote) elected conservative Sebastián Piñera into the presidency in 2010. But even then, the Concertación returned to power with Michelle Bachelet of the Chilean Socialist Party four years later.

Throughout the 1990s centrist governments of all stripes came to power, but the power they wielded in their state, and the independent space they occupied, was increasingly reduced. As unemployment remained high and economies stagnated, populations began to look for more radical solutions beyond the usual two party state represented by some version of "conservative" or "liberal," neither of which showed any distinction beyond mere style. Governments of the center-left and center-right, no matter on what promises they ran their electoral campaigns, continued to implement the programs of the Washington Consensus, with its policy known as "neoliberalism."

Out of this hopeless morass dominated by the Two Party system there began to emerge new forces on which the people began to pin their hopes. In some cases the new parties were either reformed guerrilla organizations that had become electoral parties, like the Sandinista National Liberation Front (FSLN) in Nicaragua, or the Farabundo Marti National Liberation Front (FMLN) in El Salvador. In other cases they were center-left coalitions like the aforementioned Concertación in Chile, which included the Socialists, Communists and other left parties (though a number of them defected soon after the Concertación came to power) or the coalition of the Broad Front (Frente Amplio, FA) in Uruguay. Still other parties were formed as electoral vehicles for particular candidates that represented populist projects. These included Evo Morales with the Bolivian Movement toward Socialism or MAS, the Alianza PAIS (Country Alliance) of Rafael Correa in Ecuador, the Movement of the Fifth Republic (MVR) of Hugo Chávez in Venezuela, although Chávez would later "rebrand" his party the United Socialist Party of Venezuela (PSUV).

These "Pink Tide" governments that began to win elections one after another throughout Central and South America were by no means radical but rather represented populist or social democratic projects or simply "capitalism with a human face." Nevertheless, in the context of a virulent neoliberal capitalism promoted under the rubric of the "Washington Consensus," and imposing itself at a planetary level, the "pink" governments certainly represented a post-neoliberal phase of capitalism, or at the very least, a respite from it.

By comparison with the military dictatorships or "death squad" governments of yesteryear, the Pink Tide governments could even be celebrated. Yet within Latin America, those in the social movements have become increasingly clear about the limitations of the rulers that have come to power over the past twenty-five years. They have welcomed the new wave of political leaders much the way much of the US left welcomed the Democrat Obama after two terms of George W. Bush: with a mixture of relief, apprehension and with time, growing disgust. As an Ecuadoran social movement activist told me one day in 2008 when I was visiting Quito, "Correa isn't what we want. But he's a step closer, and that's the best you can say for him."

The central problem with all of these new governments has been their acceptance of the extractivist development model, which already demonstrated itself, over the course of centuries, to be a dead-end. Now it has re-emerged under the rubric of "neo-extractivism," rhetorically framed by the progressive governments as "south-south cooperation," given that China is increasingly taking over the role of the "extractor" as US influence wanes in the region.

Under the "new" model the state often partners with international companies to undertake the digging, drilling, deforestation, or planting and harvesting of monocultures. Sometimes the extraction process has been nationalized and is carried on by the state, as in the case of Venezuela with PDVSA (Venezuelan Oil S.A.), although even there the billions that company has taken in loans from Chevron and China, the latter payable in future sales of oil, indicate a new round of dependency. [28] Sadly, even the nominal nationalization of some of these extractive industries doesn't bring the disasters to an end: it only means that now Ecuador's nationalized oil company, Petroecuador instead of Chevron spills its oil in Ecuadorean rivers.[29]

The development policies adopted by the Pink Tide governments and the governments of the right alike are not only disastrous and unsustainable, but in many cases, they aren't even profitable as the amount of money brought in from mining is often negligible. In Nicaragua, for instance, where the red and black colors of the Sandinistas are now pink, and Daniel Ortega, the aging *caudillo*, is balder, older and more neoliberal, gold has replaced cattle as the number one export of the country. Yet very little of the wealth it generates remains in Nicaragua, which only receives .06% of the gold wealth, as 99.94% leaves the country. What remains represents only 2.5% of Gross Domestic Product.[30]

Certainly, some of the income from mining, drilling, monoculture (particularly of GMO soy), lumber, etc. go to fund welfare programs to increase nutrition, health and education among those most in need, and that is certainly better than the pittance neoliberal governments threw at the social debt. But the welfare programs based on the extractive industries raise serious questions. First, are the welfare policies sustainable? What will happen to them, and to the people they benefit, when the soil, the forests and the minerals are depleted? Is welfare a "development plan"?

And there are other serious problems that come from basing an economy on the extraction of resources, including the "resource curse." Anthony Bebbington summarizes the perspectives on the problem clearly:

> Proponents of [the resource curse] thesis, or variants of it, suggest that natural resource abundance generates a series of economic and political distortions that ultimately undermine the contributions of extractive industry to development. Even authors who do not claim the existence of such a curse nonetheless argue that Latin America's relationship with resource extraction has demonstrated a "particularly virulent strain of dependency"... and that, even if the resource curse is not a generalized phenomenon, it is the case that the "twentieth century offered many opportunities for natural resource-based growth that Latin America systematically missed."[31]

The social movements of Latin America are clear that the impact the extractive activities on their countries have been, or in the near future will become, catastrophic. And they know the difference between welfare, patronage, clientelism, political demagogues who have appropriated revolutionary symbols, and that other "possible world" proclaimed by the World Social Forum, the one for which they struggle. And real social movement activists, in contrast with state-supported "movements," are clear that the only possibility for attaining that possible world is through autonomy because autonomy

...democratizes society; it dissipates centralized power; it tends toward equality; and it makes possible individuals becoming social "subjects" (actors, not objects) who participate actively in the autonomous project. Who has the right to autonomy? Everyone who demands it.[32]

Some social movement theorists have pointed out that social movements rely on liberal civil rights to emerge and grow, and "rights to assembly, association and speech [matter] especially." Where these rights are curtailed, "social movements generally decline."[33]

That autonomy and the knowledge gained from it have become dangerous to act on under the governments of the Pink Tide, just as it had been, and still is, under the governments of the right. Those in social movements who refuse to compromise or sell out to power are often categorized as "enemies" or "agents of imperialism" and face the wrath of the rulers. They are attacked with the rhetoric of the left, but from a position we ordinarily associate with the "right." This is particularly true in those countries of the Pink Tide perceived as "more radical," like Bolivia, Ecuador and Venezuela, whose turn to the left has been instigated by populist leaders.

In Bolivia Evo Morales has had problematic relations with the social movements that brought him to power. Even among the Aymara and Quechua tensions have arisen over MAS' attempts to co-opt movements or sow dissent so as to break up their power. As Julia Ojeda put it, "[Evo's MAS] has penetrated certain organizations and divided them. They enter these social movement spaces and create divisions by forming their own parallel organizations." [34] In September 2011 Evo was forced to back down on a scheme for a proposed highway through Isiboro Sécure National Park and Indigenous Territory (TIPNIS) only after over 500 of his national police attacked indigenous protesters and seriously injured 54 people on the march. Since that time, people of the Yuracaré, Moxeño and Chimán communities continue to face judicial proceedings and harassment.

In the case of Ecuador, independent movements have for years faced the insults of President Rafael Correa who refers to both the left and the indigenous people who dare to challenge his extractivist populist policies as "infantile." But they also face physical attacks and charges of "terrorism" for resisting oil drilling on indigenous lands. Marc Becker analyzes this problem adeptly, saying, "A constant difficulty for social-movement activists has been challenging Correa from the left without strengthening a common enemy on the right." [35]

But the situation isn't very different in social democratic processes, as in Brazil under the Worker's Party. There, by 1989 activists had defeated proposals to build the Belo Monte dam that would have devastated "an area of over 1,500 square kilometers of Brazilian rainforest while resulting in the forced displacement of between 20,000 - 40,000 people."[36] The plans to build the dam were revived by the Worker's Party government of Lula and the government has a 77.5% share in the project.

And when we take a close look at the situation in Venezuela a little later, we'll see the most severe contradictions of all, which help clarify more of the complex regional situation.

Anti-Imperialism and/or Solidarity

Both the changed international context and the reality on the ground in Latin America require that solidarity and transnational social justice activists do a deep reassessment of their ideas and ideologies. I think the new situation requires that we begin by distinguishing the actors in Latin America and clarify what relations we wish to have with them.

It should be evident by now that the interests of the state and those who control it, are generally distinct from the interests of the people. At times, such as in the revolutionary moment, the interests can converge and unite in a powerful combustion. But these are only moments and they pass very quickly. In normal day-to-day life, people the world over are quite clear that their interests and those of the state are not only distinct, but often at odds.

We have passed from the Revolutionary anti-colonial struggle that characterized the twentieth century and are now in a new time. The moment of confluence of interests of the people and their "vanguard" which took state power has passed. We who lived through those struggles and tasted the excitement and elation that went with it, also have a clear understanding of its cost: millions of lives, great treasure wasted to make bullets, and in the end, those vanguard parties, where they remained in power, became a new, oppressive ruling class.

No amount of denial can hide this fact if we look honestly at the legacies of Robert Mugabe, the doddering dictator of Zimbabwe; Muammar Gaddafi who ended his rule referring to his rebellious subjects as "rats" he would hunt down;

Fidel and Raul Castro, still clinging to power in a family dynasty 55 years after their revolution – and then there's the "Kim" dynasty of North Korea. In Nicaragua Daniel Ortega has returned to power as the *caudillo* or strong man of a neoliberalized Sandinista National Liberation Front.

If in the past we readily offered our solidarity to such people, their parties and their states, today we have to rethink those commitments, especially given that the current crop of governments came to power through the electoral route and govern according to that logic. Even if we feel sympathy to a particular state or political party (as some US activists sympathize with the Democrats here), it's more important than ever to affirm the need for independent, critical social movements to move those governments and parties to implement policies protective of the earth and its ecosystems, including the human ecosystem, society. Karl Polanyi made clear in his masterpiece, *The Great Transformation*, when he called for a countermovement to "re-embed the markets" in a society, when that society and, indeed, the world, have been increasingly embedded in the markets. Only critical social movements will make a demand for transformation – in the U.S., in Latin America and the world.

Historically, our anti-imperialist movement was also a solidarity movement. That is, it took on both the political and social struggles together: the political struggle against imperial domination through the colonial state (or by direct administration) and for an independent national state; and the social struggle of solidarity with the target population for their welfare, health, and self-determination. Of course, the struggle often wasn't so conceptualized at the time because, in fact, few

61

saw the distinctions between the interests of the people and the interests of those who would become "the state," that is, the political class, often organized as a vanguard party.

This was especially true in the struggles of the Central American solidarity movement in the 1980s. It was believed by many that the new state would not govern the people, but rather would be governed *by* the people: that "true, revolutionary" democracy would emerge to replace the bourgeois democracy, or the totally undemocratic dictatorship. The magical belief was commonly held that the vanguard elite that took power, and the people under its command would be transmogrified by the "Revolution" allowing the people to somehow be in power, governing an obedient vanguard that continued only to point the direction toward the promised land. In other words, there was no distinction made between parties, states and people. They were all lumped together under an idealized national or party identity.

As we'll see in the next section of this book, that conception of solidarity, formed in Leninism and applied during much of the 20th century is still very much alive. The mystique of the so-called "Bolivarian Revolution" has worked its power on much of the left in the United States and much of the world, for a long time mesmerizing even this writer. We need to draw back the curtains of the Bolivarian wizard and examine what's behind the elevated rhetoric to make a sober assessment of its actual processes, achievements or failures. That's the first step to conducting the long overdue open, respectful, but critical dialogue on what we can learn from Venezuela.

Part Two:
Bolivarian Venezuela

Socialism, Populism
or a Hybrid Regime?

Some of the issues we've been examining up to now become quite clear when we look at Venezuela, since many believe that "Venezuela represents the most far-reaching process of social transformation of the twenty-first century so far."[37] Controversy swirls around the country like no place else (contrast the perception of Uruguay, for example, viewed by many as a nice little non-controversial country even if run by a former Tupamaro guerrilla leader). It seems analysts of Venezuela can't agree on how to describe its political process or explain where it's going.

Untangling ourselves from the "belimed twigs" so as to see clearly the commonality in the processes taking place in various Latin America countries today is complex and difficult. The propaganda from all sides is sometimes so confusing that it's impossible to extricate one's self. Most listen to their spokespersons or trusted sources, but this uncritically closed loop is also dangerous, as it tends to create echo chambers in which misperceptions, false narratives, ill-founded factoids and rumors reinforce each other to create a fictitious parallel "reality" entirely detached from the actual world.

We only need to look back into recent history, some of it outlined here, to see the results of uncritical acceptance of "trusted sources." Two brief examples of this, I believe, will suffice. First, there were those who thought tales of purges, concentration camps, mass starvation and horrible cruelty under Stalin to be just the propaganda of the "capitalist press." They were slapped awake by none other than Nikita Khrushchev, yet many still maintain, decades later, that the horror was exaggerated.

Others, including even Noam Chomsky, considered early reports of mass extermination under the Khmer Rouge to be "exaggerated." Malcolm Caldwell's story is a morality tale that we would do well to consider in this context. Some will recall him as a person "well in the mainstream" of "progressive liberal thinking." Caldwell was "a history lecturer at the School of Oriental and African Studies at the University of London" and described by journalist Andrew Anthony as a "leading voice in the anti-Vietnam War campaign... and a stalwart supporter of liberation movements in the developing world." Like many others, especially on the Maoist left, Caldwell was prevented by his own ideological blinders from seeing the brutality and inhumanity of the Khmer Rouge, and thus like others, became an unwitting collaborator with genocide. Caldwell's story came to an end in Cambodia where he was murdered by Pol Pot under circumstances that remain unclear to this day. [38]

Certainly there is no regime among Latin America's "left" governments today that matches the level of criminality of regimes like Pol Pot's, and there's no reason to think any would be able or willing to exercise such extremes of repression. Nevertheless, these extreme examples raise questions about the stance left activists in solidarity with people's struggles should take, and warn us to be always alert and critical.

So in unraveling the processes taking place in Latin America since the beginning of the millennium, and taking a closer look in particular at Venezuela, it seems a good idea to again start by defining our terms or avoid terms we, for one reason or another, are unable to define.

Writers like Roger Burbach, Michael Fox and Federico Fuentes in their book, *Latin America's Turbulent Transitions: The Future of Twenty-First Century Socialism* (2013, Zed Books) at least attempt to begin with definitions. They use the word "socialism" to describe the governments of South America, in particular, Bolivia, Ecuador and Venezuela. They begin a definition of what has been called "Socialism of the Twenty-First Century" (STFC) by contrasting it with the twentieth century's "real socialism." According to the authors, STFC is defined as "rejecting authoritarianism, bureaucratic centralized planning, state capitalism and the lack of democracy." They go on to positively define STFC as that which "is built by social movements and by people organizing from below; it does not arise from government fiats nor from self-defined vanguard parties."[39]

Burbach and his fellow writers at times ignore their own working definition as they explore the processes in the "most radical" left countries of Latin America; at other times they simply ignore the features that don't fit the definition. This is particularly true as they discuss Venezuela. Examples in their Venezuela chapter abound, making it impossible to point out all of them, so we'll just look at pages 61-62.

On page 61 we read that "two million hectares of state-owned land had been redistributed by the end of 2004" and "cultivated land increased from 1.6 million hectares in 1998 to more than two million in 2006, but remained below 1980s levels." They go on to explain the results of land reform and redistribution. "Despite dramatic increases in agricultural funding, production in the countryside was unable to keep up with sharply rising consumption levels. Moreover, the combination of price and currency controls acted as a disincentive for local production as it was cheaper to import than produce locally."

It must be pointed out that the price and currency controls were government policies, which in this case, entirely undermined the government's stated goal of making the country self-sufficient in agriculture. This latter was part of a plan for "endogenous development," Hugo Chávez's early attempt to implement some form of ISI. It was a great idea, but like most of his great ideas, it went nowhere due to lack of follow-through, ineptitude in implementation, corruption and impunity, as well as, in this case, policies that were at cross-purposes.

In fact, agricultural production has been steadily declining since Chávez first came to power, as has every other industry in the country, including oil production. According to economist Anabella Abadi M., "between 1999 and 2012 food and agricultural items imported into the country grew 366%. Sadder still is the fact that coffee, corn and rice, crops that Venezuela had itself sown on 621,456.5 hectares of land in ten countries, by 2012 had to be imported."[40]

And the situation worsened in 2013. According to a report drawn from the Venezuelan daily *Ultimas Noticias,* in March 2014 imports of food had increased 51%, "of which 87.52% was purchased on international markets (about

4,298,196 tons) and only 12.48% (612,993 tons) came from local producers." [41] As for the expropriated lands intended to serve endogenous development, they have been for the most part left idle, or in some cases cannibalized. The opposition paper, *El Universal*, reports that in the case of the Hato El Porvenir commune, "The leaders of some communal organizations, like the so-called 'Peasant Socialist Communes,' allegedly steal goods from expropriated productive estates that are later sold to the mafias and then taken to Colombia." [42] The report is worth reading in its entirety.

Burbach and his fellow writers go on to talk about the cooperatives, telling us that, "between 1998 and 2005 the number of cooperatives rose from fewer than one thousand to more than seventy thousand." Quoting Camila Piñeiro Harnecker, they point out that it was "public policies that have fostered their growth." On page 62 the writers mention that in 2007 184,000 cooperatives were officially registered, but "only about 30,000, or 15 percent, were active."

The writers don't offer any explanation and in the context of a "socialist revolution" this appears to be very strange. We'll return to this a little later when we attempt our own definition of the "Bolivarian Revolution," but for now, suffice it to say that it was the "public policies" themselves that were behind the demise of the cooperatives. Cooperatives simply can't be organized "from above," and when their members don't receive adequate training and support, they're bound to fail.[43] It is generally acknowledged in Venezuela, even among Chavistas, that the attempts to build the STFC on the basis of the cooperatives was an enormous waste of money and a near-total failure.

The authors of *Latin America's Turbulent Transitions* go on to the next plan for the construction of STFC: co-management of the industries. They tell us that, "in 2005, Chávez encouraged workers to occupy their factories and run them cooperatively or in *cogestion* [co-management] with the state." By the end of 2006, the authors acknowledge, "factories under cogestion, numbered fewer than forty." They go on to admit that, "Serious problems emerged in the state-owned companies, which had been working toward cogestion."

Indeed, as Damian Prat points out in his book, *Guayana: El Milagro Al Reves* (Guayana: The Miracle in Reverse) every one of the industries in Venezuela's industrial heartland of Guayana that were nationalized from 2007 on were producing at between 20-50% of their pre-nationalized levels by 2012.[44] The situation has only worsened since Chávez's death.

And there were other problems with cogestion and its corollary, "worker control." *Cogestion* came to be viewed by many in the independent workers' unions of Guayana's Basic Industries as a method for breaking union strength. Union organizer Orlando Chirino told us that, "what they [Chávez government] called 'worker control' has been a big farce, because what the government tried to impose with 'worker control' was controlled workers."[45]

Chirino echoed the sentiments of workers in the Basic Industries whom I interviewed in in April and November 2013, saying that the Bolivarian government is "a government that calls itself socialist and pro-worker with its words, but by its acts it is an anti-union, anti-worker government that violates union freedom, imprisons leaders who resist, brings judicial proceedings against others, fires them, and ignores orders to reinstate workers."[46]

Given all of this, it might be worthwhile to revisit the definition of "socialism"! In each of the cases noted above, the initiative for the policies came from Chávez, ordered from his position of power, a pattern that certainly fits the twentieth century variant of "authoritarianism, bureaucratic centralized planning." In Venezuela, the nationalization of industries seemed more in keeping with "state capitalism."

It must be noted that the industries where Chirino and other workers were, or are, employed are run, almost entirely by active and retired military generals, which could certainly support their characterization as "lacking democracy." On the other hand, we see no evidence here of anything "built by social movements and by people organizing from below." Everything so far, in fact, arose quite directly "from government fiats" and "self-defined vanguard parties."

To call Venezuela "socialist" doesn't pass the "laugh test" in Venezuela these days, even among many Chavistas. Despite the nationalizations, the land take-overs, the laudable increase in social services, the bulk of the economy, such as it is, remains in private hands.

Certainly, the Bolivarian government fits the profile of "real" or "command" socialism that collapsed with the USSR in 1990, and it could rightly be called a "hybrid regime," but I would argue that it better fits into the category of "populism."

Kenneth Roberts lists five traits of populism:

1. A personalist and paternalistic model, increasingly charismatic and based on leadership

2. A multiclass political coalition concentrated in the lower social sectors

3. A process of political mobilization directed from above to below that skips the institutional mechanisms of mediation or subjects them to more direct ties of the leader with the people.

4. An amorphous or eclectic ideology expressed in a discourse that exalts the subalterns or is anti-elite.

5. An economic project that uses redistributive or clientelist methods on a massive scale so as to build a material base so as to gain the backing of the popular sector.[47]

While Venezuela is not, as the extreme sectors of the opposition claim, in the throes of a "dictatorship," Javier Corrales and Michael Penfold qualify it as a "hybrid regime," which they tell us, is a political system "in which the mechanism for determining access to state office combines both democratic and autocratic practices." The "key feature of hybrid regimes... is the use of legal and illegal mechanisms to erode checks and balances on the executive branch."[48] Other "factors and tools" of hybrid regimes are "packing state offices... with avowed loyalists... Badmouthing the opposition as disloyal, antidemocratic, oligarchic, antipatriotic and so forth... Excluding the opposition systematically from policy negotiations... shrinking the size of privately owned media... Invoking the law and discretionary measures to penalize opponents and offering impunity to government officials and regime-friendly business interests... Mobilizing pro-government voters in elections and using social policy as a vote-buying mechanism... Bypassing the authority of subnational officials elected by the opposition and limiting their share of state revenue... expanding the prerogatives of the military and liberating them from the scrutiny of civilian authorities other than the executive branch."

We'll see in the following pages a few examples of these traits offered by Corrales and Penfold, traits that fit the Bolivarian process that is marketed to the world as "socialist" and a "Revolution." And if the Bolivarian government has been successful at anything, it's been at marketing. After all, for the president of a country that produces the highest amount of carbon in Latin America, whose primary export is oil, whose government subsidizes gas to the extent that it is the cheapest in the world, to describe that country's "Revolution" as "ecosocialist" and have a significant portion of the intelligentsia and the left accept the statement in all seriousness, is marketing that outdoes Madison Avenue.[49]

"Economic Warfare"
We have seen the Enemy and he is Us
Pogo

How has Venezuela come to the verge of collapse when prices for its crude oil are at historic highs, ranging from $90 to over $100/barrel? First, the problem is precisely the oil and its impact on countries with the "resource curse." Terry Karl writes that, "Oil booms seem to promise the opportunity for real choice and for the alteration of a development trajectory. But when they occur in countries with a legacy of oil-led development, especially a decision-making apparatus dependent on petrodollars, choice is in fact quite narrow... booms generate powerful and even overwhelming incentives to sustain existing trajectories but on a grander, more accelerated, and ultimately unmanageable scale. Thus they are the catalyst for future trouble." [50] Margarita López Maya, Venezuelan historian and sociologist adds to this that, "Petro-states tend to act with few and weak institutional checks and balances, and as a result they are prone to administrative inefficiency and corruption."[51]

According to Corrales and Penfold, the hybrid regime of Venezuela has burned through this oil money "recycling" ISI policies which have "led to extraordinary inefficiencies and, once again, to an expansion rather than a contraction of imports." [52] The "extraordinary inefficiencies" are reflected in the economy in a number of ways. Venezuela has been hit in the past year with shortages, high inflation, balance of payment problems, and bond yields at levels reserved for failed states.

In January 2014, even before the student demonstrations rocked the country, bond yields were as high as 16%, the highest in Latin America. By contrast, the Ukraine's bonds were 11%.[53] The bonds have vacillated over time, but have rarely gone below 10%. The economic disaster currently afflicting Venezuela has been blamed by President Nicolás Maduro and the Chavistas on "economic warfare" although, like the dozen or so alleged assassination plots the president also claims are in the works to eliminate him, no evidence to back up the claim is ever forthcoming – unless evidence the government itself apparently forged counts.[54]

Corruption was and is a major problem in the Bolivarian government, and the issues around the $29 billion unaccounted for in the FONDEN development fund, personally overseen by Chávez, are just the tip of the iceberg.[55] More serious is the enormous amount of money that has disappeared to shell businesses manipulating the huge gap between the official rate and the black market rate for goods.[56] The government policies of "currency control" are a seemingly infinite source of corruption,[57] the creation of parallel (or "black") markets, trafficking, contraband and every other kind of marginal activity.

It's one of the vexing problems of any attempt at building "socialism," or even a welfare system based on subsidies, price controls, and other measures designed to subvert the market, that the Market is always just across the river or the other side of the bridge in the other country. Flour or milk under price controls on one side of a border quickly find their market value on the other side, and there's always someone available to offer transport for the difference in price. The island of socialism in a sea of capitalism can work if there are no rafts or bridges to the mainland, or if the distance separating the two can't be somehow navigated. Cuba is evidence of that, if what they've been doing on that island for the past fifty or so years can be called "socialism" rather than "state capitalism."[58]

But when your border can be crossed by hopping from rock to rock, or by paddling a canoe, or walking a log, or even just crossing a bridge with an extra tank jury-rigged on the car to carry the gas, or by bribing a National Guard official (the most common way in Venezuela), the leak in the dike isn't capable of being plugged with a single finger, or probably even many thousands.

Such is the case with Venezuela. Around this problem of smuggling and contraband and the lure of distant markets where fabulous profits can be made beyond the borders of the utopia of "socialism," all this is only part of the problem, pointing to a deeper and more baffling question. One must walk very carefully when tampering with the market, as any politician, left or right, will tell you, since this mechanism is, like it or not, is the adjudicator of "value."

Aristotle considered this fact as he puzzled over the question of a pair of shoes and left the question unanswered as a Rubiks cube for future generations to solve. David Hawkes says that in a sense the strange problem of the use and exchange value of a pair of shoes that perplexed the great thinker became a core problem for philosophy in the west for the next twenty or so centuries, and was taken up by Marx as a central concern in *Capital*. In the words of Aristotle,

Every possession has a double use. Both of these uses belong to it as such, but not in the same

74

way, the one being proper and the other not proper to the thing. In the case of footwear, for example, one can wear it or one can exchange it. (*Politics* 1257a, 7–10)

Hawkes goes on to clarify the problem:

The shoe is then not simply a shoe, it must be conceived as equivalent to the object for which it is to be exchanged. We must impose an idea on the object which does not naturally belong to its material properties. For this to be possible on any large scale, a common denominator is necessary. We need a sphere of representation which can mediate between the shoe in itself and our idea of the shoe. According to Aristotle, this medium is money. [59]

Although Hawkes might not want to acknowledge it (or at least not in a phone interview with this writer), when you mess with prices, you mess with "value." A zero price tag equates in the consumer mind to zero value – and who, in the modern capitalist world economy isn't a consumer? Perhaps a few uncontacted tribes have managed to avoid the mass insanity and irrationalism of the market mind, but they are rare, indeed.

And what even Aristotle failed to take into account was a third set of values, which we might call the "original" or, my friend Kevin Rath calls "intrinsic," value, since nothing comes from nothing and all "commodities" have an "original" value before they underwent the process of "manufacturing." What value, in the case of the shoes, did the leather have to the cow from which

75

it came? Obviously a sight more than its "use" value as a pair of shoes, much less its "exchange" value in the market. What is the value of an old tree in the forest? Is it measured in "board feet" or for the thousands of "uses" it has to birds, squirrels, insects, bacteria, fungi, and even the forest and land itself as it maintains its own integrity by maintaining the integrity of the whole? How does one go about "quantifying" that value in dollars and cents, and is it even possible?

This question, more than any other, it seems to me, is the reason humanity still hasn't closed the book on the idea of an alternative: call it socialism, communism, anarchism or whatever. Nor should it. Capitalism, in the end, clearly doesn't have all, or even most, of the answers. That's why the socialist revolutions, anarchist struggles and the Bolivarian process itself have arisen over the past couple of centuries to challenge this economic system.

While it may initially seem to be a great digression from our subject of Venezuela to be talking about three sets of values, the idea of "value" is at the very core of anything touching on a process, the professed aim of which is to develop "socialism" (command economies) or the STFC. It's no exaggeration to say that the STFC, the Missions that Chávez designed, ostensibly to bring Venezuela out of poverty, all this seems to be foundering on the very attempt to redefine "value" and wrest control of its definition from the hands of the Market. It's something the Soviet Union failed to do, and they did it with far greater minds, a far more committed and disciplined party, and far more consistently than Venezuela has done. And the Soviet Union failed. And I would argue that it failed precisely on this very problem.

In Venezuela, a bag of flour has use value for someone who cooks, but one can only cook and eat so much flour. In an economy where money loses value measurably on a weekly basis due to inflation (Venezuela has the highest inflation of Latin America, and among the highest in the world, coming in at around 60% in 2013), the subsidized sack of flour has a much greater "value" as exchange, especially if the exchange can be made on the Colombian side of the border. So smuggling contraband from one side of the border to the other is a big business in the region, so much so that it has nearly official status.

Connected with this, and taking place across Venezuela, especially among those with a little bit of extra cash is "speculation" on commodities. Again, due to the high inflation resulting from an economy dependent almost entirely on imports, saving money is rationally a bad investment strategy, unless the money happens to have a US president on it. What the government calls "speculation" (that is, investing in products and holding them until the prices rise) is what any rational Venezuelan with a little bit "money lite" in the form of bolos would call "rational investment." If you have a business, for instance, and you know that over the next year you'll sell $100 worth of toilet paper, it makes sense to buy it now in bolívares since the value of the toilet paper will go up just as surely as the value of the bolívar will go down, given the present regime's monetary policies. This is even more true if you have to import the toilet paper, which in Venezuela will almost certainly be the case. Here the profit in "speculation" is multiplied many times by the government's policy of currency control.

Currency controls were implemented to prevent capital flight as the government policies changed and many Venezuelan businesses decided to leave the country and take the money with them. Suddenly they found they couldn't take the money with them, or rather convert their money once they left. This had the effect of keeping capital in the country. Or so the theory goes. As with most "solutions," it also creates several more problems, many of them more serious than the original one the "solution" attempted to fix.

Under currency control the CADIVI (Commission for the Administration of Currency Exchange) fixed the rate of exchange of dollars to *bolívares* (commonly shortened to *bolos*, the national money of Venezuela) at 4.3 to one US dollar, a rate that rose to 6.3 after the February 2013 devaluation. Importers, then, would buy dollars at that rate to import, in our example, the toilet paper. So far, so good. Given that some 80% of goods now consumed in Venezuela are imported, our "speculator" would have to be licensed to import and get that rate. There would be strong motivation to do so, even with all the red tape since this rate is far below the "real market" (that is, the "black market" in Cúcuta, Colombia, in the casas de cambio, or money exchanges) which now reach up to fifteen times that "official" value.

And so it is no surprise, as Mayela Armas H. noted that, in 2012, 27.4% of all imports were "fictitious."[60] This would mean that more than a quarter of that $100 our imaginary "speculator" received from his bolos to buy toilet paper didn't buy toilet paper. What did he or she buy? With the black market rate (at the time of this writing, and rising as I type this sentence) at 87.82 bolos to the dollar (the very next night, as I revised this, it was nearly 1 bolo higher), it's easy to figure out where $27.40 would likely go: right into the black market to buy bolos. Rounding up that black market price, that's 2,411 bolos that our speculator just purchased for under thirty dollars, representing $383 US and change, at the official rate. So now our speculator has $72.60 worth of toilet paper that he or she can mark up the value to black market prices (about 15 times), because everyone knows that markets, not governments, set prices, no matter what laws and regulations might be passed, and that's particularly true in Venezuela at this moment. So suddenly, voila! He/she now has $72.60 worth of toilet paper (at the official rate) and 2,411 bolos in the pocket, having started out with the modest sum of 630 bolos to buy the initial $100. Now this is the kind of "socialism" our speculator likes! The profits beat a capitalist system hands down! And this is how $69 billion dollars has been lost to Venezuela in ten years of currency control, which was ostensibly a system for preventing just such a bleeding.[61]

Not surprisingly, according to Armas, among official entities, the rate of false billings is higher, coming in at 39.7%. Let's round that off to 40% just to make life easier, and it becomes clear how the currency is being controlled and in whose interest. The "who" might well be, and likely are, the people who designed this system in the first place, since most designers of economic systems usually design them to benefit themselves.

This seems to be the case in Venezuela, according to Mario Silva. In the secret meeting the popular Chavista talk-show host of the "Razor's Edge" (La Hojilla) talked about the President of the National Assembly and high-ranking PSUV member Diosdado Cabello to a Cuban intelligence agent. The conversation was recorded and later leaked by the opposition, and it's a revealing portrayal of the inner workings of a degenerate "revolutionary" party, and one that makes the Sandinista "piñata" look like a children's party.[62] Silva pointed specifically to Cabello's involvement in these scams when he mentioned "the flight of capital through firms, some of them front firms, some others in line with Diosdado Cabello, through Cadivi. The allocation of foreign currency that went out and intended, put it in inverted commas, to make deals of private businesses and it turned out that they would spend a portion and sell the remaining portion. There was flight of capital and this caused the exaggerated difference between the price at [VEB] 4.30 and the other price," the other price, of course, being the black market price.

Every so often the government puts out another currency control system designed to "stop the corruption" but the designers, and their friends, always build in back doors to take the money out in wheelbarrows. Now, for instance, there is SICAD2 in which the dollars go up for auction and are usually sold for half the black market rate, but considerably higher than the "official" rate the government gives tourists who change, or sell dollars to "preferred" or "strategic" sectors of the economy.

There's another complication to this economic mess, and that is the issue of price controls, which is where we began this subject. To keep the cost of basic necessities in reach of the average Juan Bimbo (Joe Anyone), the government implements a ceiling on the prices vendors can legally charge for products. There are several problems with this "solution," as we saw earlier.

First, given the rate of inflation, the limits are quickly unfeasible given the costs of production requires local production be done at a loss. The government ends up importing food and paying a higher price for it than if it were locally produced (if there were no price/currency controls), and then subsidizing the price to make the food affordable. As one Venezuelan complained to me, "they import chicken from Brazil and subsidize it so that the price is lower in Venezuela than it is in Brazil." It's no surprise, then, that this food then becomes contraband, sometimes returning to its country of origin that, due to the government subsidy, becomes very profitable, undercutting its original price.

The other problem is that with the Fair Price Law, decreed in January 2014, no one is really clear exactly how profit is determined in such a distorted economy. How does one assess costs and by which monetary exchange system? Does unremunerated labor figure into the equation when people are forced to fill out many forms, visit and bribe the right officials to get imported raw materials in a manufacturing process? And what about the bribes: are they figured in as a "business expense"? As often happens in Venezuela, the law will be aimed at perceived "enemies of the Revolution" and a few sacrificial Bolivarian lambs to give the appearance of "equal justice before the law." But the law will certainly have a chilling effect on business and this, along with the normal difficulties of obtaining foreign exchange at preferential rates, will lead to more empty shelves and more businesses closing across the country.[63]

Nevertheless, despite all these problems and complex and intractable contradictions Venezuela was the only country in the new millennium that was challenging capitalism as a system and proposing a new model of society against the dominant neoliberalism foisted on the world by the USA. That was a good thing, right? But the Venezuelan model didn't seem to be working any better. In fact, in many ways, it has been functioning far worse. The government has been "curing" itself with the medieval solution to the problem of inflation, with price controls. It has also been financing its own bleeding, the leeches firmly planted all over its body, now slowly sucking it dry.

Development through Nationalizations?

In the 2007 "Social and Economic Plan of the Nation" Chavez "contemplated the nationalization of all the strategic sectors of the national economy."[64] Accordingly, by 2012 some 1,087 businesses and industries had been nationalized, nearly 500 in 2012 alone.

One of those strategic industries was cement. According to "el Comandante Presidente" Chávez, it was preferable to have the state control all the cement production rather than three multinationals which controlled 75% of the market. [65] "One of the problems," Chávez explained," is that many times here we've had to paralyze construction of housing because there isn't enough cement and whatever there is is very expensive" and moreover, "these companies export cement out of the country when we need it here to build housing, universities, Bolivarian schools, highways, etc."

Today it's nearly impossible to find cement in the country. One of the reasons for the scarcity is that the price is regulated, and when products are regulated, they're prime targets for speculation and trafficking out of the country, as in the case of the "mafia of the steel rods" in Guayana.[66] The other reason is that, in keeping with the general, one is tempted to say "universal," trend of the nationalized industries, production of cement is down to 30%[67] or even 20% of what it was under the three multinationals that produced it before. The same is true for steel, smelting coke, and other products once made in Venezuela's industrial heartland of Guayana. [68] The other nationalized industries of Guayana in the State of Bolívar have also performed poorly under the management of a corrupt and incompetent state bureaucracy. Sidor, or Siderúrgica del Orinoco, a steel company, was nationalized in 2008. In 2007, according to Robert Bottome of the business journal, VenEconomia, the company had produced 4.3 tons of liquid steel. By 2012 the nationalized company was down to producing 1.7 tons.

Journalist Damian Prat estimates a 70% drop in production across the board in the nationalized industries. [69] Seeing this disaster unfold, National Workers Union coordinator Marcela Máspero opined that the "government is collapsing the nationalized businesses to put them in the hands of private capital." She believes it's all part of a plan to break workers' power as the government "dismantles worker control in the state industries."[70]

The nationalizations and expropriations go a long way toward explaining the deterioration of the Venezuelan economy which dates back a number of years. Indeed, Corrales and Penfold write that, "by early 2009 the Chávez administration was in a typical collapse-phase mode."[71] At present it appears, the country is in what some have described as "Phase 3," the penultimate phase of populist cycles, described as a situation in which "pervasive shortages, extreme acceleration of inflation, and an obvious foreign exchange gap lead to capital flight and demonetization of the economy" where "the budget deficit deteriorates violently..."[72]

But there are many other factors behind the economic catastrophe. For instance, the "petro-diplomacy" of the late President Hugo Chávez has cost the country dearly. Corrales refers to some estimates that Chávez "has provided or promised as much aid to Latin American countries, in real terms, as the U.S. spent on the Marshall Plan in Europe after World War II."[73] Margarita López Maya mentions that Venezuela has given more aide in the past decade or so to Cuba than the Soviet Union had.[74]

The Bolivarian "Revolution from Above" has spent the last decade or so buying political allies from Caracas to Buenos Aires and even New York and Washington DC. It's an interesting twist that, while the US left is concerned over US attempts to fund the Venezuelan opposition, as Casto Ocando notes, "the amount of money that Chávez paid to powerful politicians, law firms, NGOs and lobbyists in the United States to promote his revolution, I discovered went over $300 million in less than a decade, much more than that which his government had accused Washington of having given to the Venezuelan opposition."[75]

This is all but an extension into the international realm of the patronage policies implemented at home. While such "internationalism" might seem admirable from the outside, it generates deep resentments inside the country, especially since "It's really in the popular (working and poor classes) zones where the economic crisis has hit with the greatest fury, pulverizing salaries and draining the markets and condemning the public and private productive apparatus to a paralysis that devastates employment and tends to inflate imports."[76]

Unfortunately, due to the fact that the government controls currency and is therefore in charge of allotting it to industries so they can purchase vital inputs for their manufacturing, the government has also been collapsing private industry at the same time that it has allowed its nationalized industries to decay.

As a result of the lack of foreign currency to pay for necessary imports, production in 2014 in big industry is working at 58.2% of capacity, while medium-sized industry is at 48.7% and small business at 44.8% of capacity. While private business still isn't at the abysmal production rates of the state industries, they're dangerously poor.

It seems that the government owes $9 billion US to industry which has to wait an average of 300 days to get its money.[77] This helps explain the shortages afflicting the country.

It also raises questions about the first of the five "revolutions" that Maduro announced with such fanfare on September 2, 2014, the " economic revolution, promoting production, 'in order to guarantee stability.'" Maduro proclaimed, "All the efforts of the government should be concentrated on this, to make this revolution successful." We'll see what he does to ensure that businesses, nationalized and private both, receive needed inputs, spare parts, in a more timely manner. I remain, along with the great majority of Venezuelans, very skeptical.

Breaking Democracy,
One Institution at a Time

Perhaps the most alarming part of Chávez's, and now Maduro's, populist program, is the co-optation of the social movements, a very common practice of populist governments. While populists have "expanded the franchise, incorporating previously excluded groups," they have "not valued the liberal traditions of civil rights and pluralism."[78] There is no question that the new wave of social movements in Latin America today has benefitted from the democratic openings that occurred from the 1990s on, but the populist projects, particularly in Venezuela, pose a threat to their growth and power. "Contrary to liberals, who argue that in a differentiated society with a plurality of interests, the will of the people cannot be conceived as one and homogeneous, populists and Marxists have understood the people as having one will."[79]

Social movements are the very embodiment of a democracy that "fulfills an essential role in holding current power holders accountable, stimulating public debate, and allowing for learning and corrections on the way."[80] For that reason, Kurt Weyland concludes that, "democracy arguably has normative priority over substantive efforts at change."[81] The Bolivarian strategy of the cooptation of social movements and projects at the community level is clear even, or perhaps especially, in those projects deemed most "democratic."

But that's not how the Bolivarian government sees things, despite its rhetoric to the contrary. It's impossible to square democracy of any kind, representative or "participatory," included, under a single leader within whose movement no one dares to challenge. Certainly Chavistas are happy to criticize the "Revolution" and the government, the party, the bureaucracy, and any number of other abstractions, but one notices among them the peculiar and absolute avoidance of even the appearance of criticism of the late "*Comandante Eterno*."

That this "Revolution" was a top-down construction of Chávez there is absolutely no doubt, despite all the claims, some of them valid, of activity from below. In Venezuela, the distinct branches of the government were consolidated and centralized under the command of Hugo Chávez, starting with the rewriting of the Bolivarian Constitution in 1999.

Allan R. Brewer-Carías, a Venezuelan with a long resumé of service as Professor of law at the Central University of Venezuela, Cambridge, Trinity College, University of Paris II, Columbia University, former senator and Minister for Decentralization in Venezuela, says that "Venezuela has an authoritarian government created not by the classic Latin American military coup d'état but rather by a systematic process of destroying from within the state all the basic principles of democracy, its institutions, and the Constitution."[82] Ironically, it was all done in the name of a "protagonistic and participatory democracy." But that cumbersome term, along with its partner, "endogenous development," have now fallen by the wayside as the process takes a sharp turn toward greater military control and authoritarian measures under Nicolas Maduro.

As Brewer-Carías has laboriously demonstrated,[83] democracy in Venezuela has been carefully deconstructed, often by use of its own tools, to construct an authoritarian state under the command of the late *caudillo*, President Hugo Chávez. All the work of decentralization done in the 1990s which enabled the left, particularly MAS (Movement toward Socialism) and Causa R to win seats, and the latter to nearly win a presidential election, the decentralization that, in fact, enabled Chávez himself to come to power, was destroyed under Chávez. His recentralization of the government and subversion of governors and mayors in opposition was part of a strategy for complete control of the country.

This strategy continues to be implemented at the time of this writing as the Bolivarian central government withholds funding for those towns and cities across the country where majorities elected opposition mayors. In some cases, like the state of Miranda, where current President Nicolás Maduro has "refused to recognize the legitimacy of [Mayor] Henrique Capriles as governor" the Bolivarians have "created 'the Miranda Corporation' that serves to operate as a parallel governing authority where they've put into command Elías Jaua, the man who lost the last elections against Capriles."[84]

This is a clear pattern in the strategy for "hegemony" drawn up under Chávez. The most notable case was that of the popular opposition mayor of Caracas, Antonio Ledezma. After winning that 2008 mayoral election against Chavista Aristobulo Isturiz, the Chavista-dominated National Assembly passed the Capital District Law which transferred money, responsibilities "and personnel of the Metropolitan Mayor of Caracas to a new Venezuelan Capital District (headed by Jacqueline Faría, an official directly appointed by Hugo Chavez)."[85] The democratically-elected Mayor of Caracas lost 90% of his budget and had his workforce cut from 17,000 to 3,000[86] with the blocking of the popular vote in the name of "participatory and protagonistic democracy" and "popular power."

The insult to the injury came from the base of the Chavista movment and it appeared to be part of a concerted effort to completely remove Ledezma from power. The new mayor soon found out that he was "not even allowed inside city hall. Soon after Ledezma was sworn in, pro-Chavez thugs occupied the ornate, colonial building, painted graffiti on the walls and urinated on the floors." He was forced to move his office, and Faría moved in.[87]

The community councils (CCs) are another good example of Chávez's strategy to build a parallel state directly under his command and gradually demolish the previous liberal democratic order behind it. In theory the CCs are examples of STFC and "popular power" (the term which has now replaced "participatory and protagonistic democracy"), but in fact they are replicating the experience of previous "movements" initiated from above by the "Comandante:" the Bolivarian Circles, the Bolivarian Electoral Battalions and so forth. They have all been characterized by "the persistence of clientelism in the exchange of social services for political support, and a charismatic style of rule that neutralizes or prevents autonomous grassroots inputs."[88] According to one member of one of the earlier autonomous neighbor's councils, grassroots organizations on which the CC were modeled, "The community councils are the perfect size to mobilize people in elections, but not to resolve problems of housing and the problems of the neighborhoods."[89]

De la Torre thinks such organizations as the CCs, Bolivarian Circles and other projects of Chávez have suffered "problems of autonomy because they were created from above."[90] None of this is to say that there was no social movement activity in Venezuela before the coming of Chávez. In fact, there was considerable social movement, community education and union activity over the years prior to the beginning of the Bolivarian process. [91] But these non-party-affiliated, autonomous social movements arising out of communities were sidelined with the coming of the Bolivarian process.

Community organizations and activists were left behind as people, particularly the poor, with few options, flocked around the better-financed activists of Chávez, flush with oil money. The "blessings" of the "resource curse" have changed the nature of "social movement" activity in Venezuela by subsidizing it. On one hand, this pattern has fed into the activation of people, thrusting them into social and political activity in favor of the Bolivarian process, but on the other hand, the new activists participate with a clear realization that there exists an invisible government line to toe if they wish to continue receiving subsidies. As in every other case of populist cooptation, organizers find themselves responding to the needs of the government over those of the community in which they work.[92]

Cooptation and winning elections was precisely the objective of the "Missions," as Chávez himself admitted. Readers will recall that the Missions were programs ostensibly designed to eliminate poverty in Venezuela. Chávez's good fortune began just months before the Referendum that looked likely to unseat him. According to

Cristina Marcano and Alberto Barrera Tyszka, with the skyrocketing price of oil set off by the US invasion of Iraq in 2003, Chávez suddenly had immense wealth from oil sales over which he had personal control. Prior to this time, Marcano and Tyszka characterized Chávez's welfare programs as "inefficient." "Indeed, they seemed a bit too similar to the previous government's programs— asphyxiated by cronyism, bureaucracy and accusations of corruption."[93]

This all changed when the money flooded in from oil sales, and Chávez was able to do an end-run around the opposition with the misiones (missions), which were a series of social programs designed to "eradicate poverty by 2021." Critics charge that these projects, including the much-touted Barrio Adentro medical clinics, Mercal supermarkets, Bolivarian schools from *Misión Robinson* through the Bolivarian universities, and many others, are

> populist, discretionary and operated without the benefit of external control. According to sociologist Luis Pedro España, the *misiones* seem designed more to help Chávez retain power than to combat poverty in Venezuela effectively. All the programs function by remitting salary grants to the participants, according to a system of partisan affiliations and loyalty to the government. Moreover, none of these programs is audited. For this reason there is no way to know how many people participate in these programs, how much is invested in them, or what kind of results they obtain. The only possible source for this information is the government itself.[94]

This latter being the case, it might be important in evaluating information about the missions to keep in mind I.F. Stone's famous and pithy axiom, "governments lie." The full quote, "All governments lie, but disaster lies in wait for countries whose officials smoke the same hashish they give out," could in this case be amended as "whose officials huff the same gas they use to buy followers."

That Chávez started the missions specifically to win the referendum against his opponents the writers of his biography leave no doubt. They tell us that, "the launch of these initiatives [*misiones*] coincided with a downward trend in Hugo Chávez's popularity ratings. The upturn was immediate." Even Chávez acknowledged this, saying,

> In 2003, they gave me a news bomb: if the referendum were held today, you would lose...That was when we started to work with the *misiones* and I began to ask Fidel [Castro] for help. He said to me, 'If there's one thing I know, it's about that kind of thing.' And we started to invent the *misiones*.[95]

But the new "revolutionary Bolivarian" state the Chavistas were trying to build isn't working well either. Problems of financing two parallel states, even if one is being gradually defunded, are beginning to show on the economy, especially given that oil production is in a state of continual decline at 3-4% per year due to deferred maintenance.[96]

While Venezuela under Chávez initially made great gains in reducing poverty, illiteracy and providing health care, subsidized food at low prices, and other social projects through the early years of the recent oil and commodities boom, there is no doubt the country is now moving backwards. Estimates indicate that Venezuelans are living by 1991 standards as the price of the basic food basket has gone up 75% between May 2013 and May 2014 and it now costs 4.6 minimum wage salaries to pay for it.[97] With the scarcity index reaching an astounding 60% in March of this year[98] (spiking from 30%, no doubt in part due to the student demonstrations and the government's response) the dissatisfaction is growing in tandem with the government's seeming inability to resolve the most basic problems of providing of food.

The same is true of the hospitals in the country. While Chávez funded Barrio Adentro clinics (under his command) he defunded the hospital system, which once offered good health care for the entire country. Now, the Venezuelan Association of Clinics and Hospitals (AVCH) has called on the National Executive to "declare a humanitarian emergency in this sector 'before the grave situation of the health system, the heightened scarcity and the irregularity of supplies, medicines, medical and surgery materials, medical equipment and replacement parts for that equipment, which puts at risk the possibility of diagnosis and the lives of sick human beings."[99]

Repression rarely took place under Chávez, or was at least selective and subtle. The more egregious violations of civil rights under the late leader generally involved the arbitrary imprisonment of high-profile, perceived enemies like Judge Maria Afiuni,[100] General Raúl Baduel (and his son, arrested in the demonstrations of Spring 2014),[101] union leaders like Rubén González (who in April 2014 was declared innocent, ending his five-year-long nightmare of imprisonment and struggle with the Venezuelan justice system),[102] Pemon and other indigenous activists.[103]

Chávez had other ways of dealing with his opponents. Among other things, he made use of the well-known tools for social control common to populist projects, in particular, depriving his enemies and opponents of the benefits of patronage. Given that oil represents 96% of exports and half of Venezuela's fiscal income,[104] the government is the largest employer and, under currency controls, the only viable source for foreign currency necessary for import or export. Being on the outs with the government can deal a severe blow to an individual's livelihood. Eliminating enemies from access to the revenue from oil, therefore, effectively closed those individuals out of the economy, and that's just what the Tascón List did.

This list, drawn up by Luis Tascón, included the names of all who had signed the 2004 Referendum against Chávez and found themselves excluded from access to work and to the government. The infamous "List," which later became the "Maisanta" program, was supposedly dropped later, but there is some question about if or when.[105]

Under Maduro, as a result of all these failed economic policies, the country has become increasingly ungovernable, people have suffered shortages, electrical blackouts and other serious problems, and the government's response has been an increasing use of violence as a means of social control. Fierce battles took place in the spring of 2014 between students and their allies on one side, and on the other, the police, military and paramilitary colectivos, the latter paramilitaries operating outside the law but "seen acting in a manner in conjunction with State security forces in violent acts of control over demonstrations or as police or military complacently looked on." [106] These conflicts turned the country into a war zone. It's also true that some in the opposition have responded violently to the repression and to many, the situation appears to be spiraling out of control. In any case, at the time of this writing in August 2014 the protests that began in February of this year are still ongoing, even if they've dropped out of the news in the US, and it's likely they'll increase as the country passes through greater economic difficulties.

While some analysts predict collapse as "imminent," Venezuela has thus far been able to prop itself up by selling its future to China in oil-for-loan agreements. This could go on for quite a while since the next elections are in 2015, and the country still has oil under the ground. Yet with a decaying infrastructure, especially in the state industries, including Petroleos de Venezuela S.A. (PDVSA), and the fact that much of the easily recoverable crude is gone, leaving primarily only heavier oil (effectively tar sands) recoverable,[107] we might see dramatic shifts in the country very soon. Indeed, at the time of this writing, it appears that Venezuela may soon begin importing oil, even though it has the world's largest reserves. [108] Scandalously, it has already been importing refined gas from the U.S. since its refinery at Amauy exploded in 2012, gas which it then subsidizes and sells for a few cents per gallon.[109]

Whatever word one might wish to use to describe the Bolivarian process, it's clear that a majority of Venezuelans no longer support the [socialist? populist? hybrid?] regime. The criminal violence that takes upwards of 15,000 lives a year (96% of which goes uninvestigated), [110] the censorship and consolidation of government "hegemony" over media[111] in addition to all the other problems detailed above have eroded most of the remaining good will of Venezuelans for the Bolivarian process. Maduro is still not reaching the depths of rejection that US leaders, the President and the Congress, for instance, are experiencing. But a 59 % disapproval rating in May 2014 is serious and his popularity hasn't increased since.[112]

Two Elites, One People

We cannot design from above a way out of this corrupt system in which people are routinely jailed for standing up for their rights... But with solidarity it is possible to save lives and create conditions for the people themselves to find a way out and solutions to problems. Never will one party, including CAUSA R, be the protagonist of change. We are in a time of new forms of struggle that require new ideas. The people will develop the way out, free of political chiefs, free of the verticalism that characterizes the so-called left in this country.[113]

Matias Carmunas

These were the words of "a priest from the working-class barrios of Petare," speaking soon after a previous round of demonstrations, riots and repression known as the "Caracazo" in 1989. They have an eerie resonance today in Venezuela, although the optimism expressed by Carmunas is now rare. As polarization in Venezuela raises fears of civil war, many on both sides are coming to recognize the situation is perpetuated and manipulated by the elites of both the PSUV and the parties of the opposition. The people, as one critical Chavista acknowledged to me, "are being used as cannon fodder for both elites."

This is also the conclusion that Venezuelans on opposite sides came to in an interview by journalist Franz von Bergen. Interviewing Julio "Coco" Jimenez, dissident of the opposition on one side and members of Marea Socialista (Socialist Tide) on the other, von Bergen begins by quoting some "one," presumably "Coco," and spotlights an area that has remained in large part ignored outside of the country but which is becoming increasing the center of attention within Venezuela. "'There's a struggle from the base toward the top,' says one. 'It's a struggle of the base against the [political] castes,' says the other." Von Bergen notes that this dissatisfaction of bases with their "castes" is the one thing that unites all Venezuelans since they see their elites "making decisions in an arbitrary manner, without respecting democratic processes."[114] "Coco" points out that the only leaders of parties democratically elected by their base are those in the Causa R (R Cause) and Voluntad Popular (Popular Will), the party of opposition leader Leopoldo Lopez. Lopez is currently imprisoned, awaiting trial for encouraging the demonstrations of February 2014.

The Pink Tide came in with the commodities boom that has taken place since the beginning of this millennium and its fortunes are tied to a great degree to Venezuela whose fortunes are tied to the most important commodity in modern civilization: oil.

The price of oil and all other commodities in a world of limited resources is volatile. Any economy dependent on the extraction of a single resource is subject to that volatility, as is its political system. In good times, governments can do what the Venezuelan government has traditionally done when it was "Venezuela Saudita:" it can spread the money around by subsidizing social programs.

Unfortunately, most governments don't invest that money coming in from commodities in productive enterprises, but rather in subsidies because subsidies buy loyalty, and loyalty means votes. That's one reason why Venezuela is in collapse mode, and other governments that have benefited from the Bolivarian prosperity by receiving cheap oil or cash, or who have followed the same path, will also suffer in the future.

As Bolivian economist Roberto Laserna points out, "though the Ecuadoran and Bolivian economies are growing, the more productive sectors that would support sustainable expansion are not. Indeed, both countries have become more exposed to global economic volatility, despite their leaders' vows to reduce dependence on the global capitalist order.[115]

Kurt Weyland writes that the "radicalism" of what he calls the "contestatory left" (meaning Bolivia, Venezuela and Ecuador) "has prevailed in

100

countries that have relied heavily on oil or gas exports, that benefited tremendously from the international price boom of recent years, and that therefore saw fiscal constraints temporarily loosened." But these governments "often mismanage the exceptional revenues produced by booms, go on ill-considered spending sprees, fail to broaden the economic base, and do not prepare for the subsequent bust bound to occur sooner or later."[116]

Those countries considered "moderate" appear to be better prepared to weather the downturn in commodity prices. Weyland says that, "the accomplishments of the moderate left stand on a more solid foundation and therefore accumulate over time – producing substantial, lasting social progress."[117]

What's Left?

The most important step now for what remains of the Latin American solidarity movement in the US and other leftists who have supported the Pink Tide governments, especially Venezuela, is to open up a discussion about who and what they support and why. Certainly we can support democratic transitions that enable greater numbers of the previously excluded to participate in politics and the economy. We can applaud such attempts, no matter how feeble or corrupt or tainted with ulterior motives. But we shouldn't avoid mentioning that they are feeble, corrupt and tainted with ulterior motives.

And when projects are feeble, corrupt, and tainted with ulterior motives, they usually don't fare well. In fact, they usually fail, sooner or later. And when they do, they debilitate future attempts to build humane projects.

Solidarity activists have historically had two very different responses to the failures of projects they supported. Not having honestly assessed those projects beforehand, some of us have tended to idealize them, view them unrealistically, and then when they unexpectedly fail, to turn our backs on them. Others have ignored inconsistencies and gone into deep denial about the failures, blaming the failure on the imperialists, the capitalists or any other handy scapegoat. Both of these positions are essentially dishonest and forms of denial.

In this regard, the studies of Festinger, Riecken and Schachter are very interesting. In their book, *When Prophesy Fails,* they examine a cult whose founder had prophesied the coming end of the world. When the expected event didn't arrive, the members reacted in various ways to the "dissonance" between the prophesy and the reality, depending on a number of factors. Because "dissonance produces discomfort," it is natural that there "will arise pressures to reduce or eliminate the dissonance."[118] This is because "the central belief and its accompanying ideology are... of crucial importance in the believer's lives and hence the dissonance is very strong – and very painful to tolerate."

Interestingly, only two of the eleven members of the cult studied by Festinger and his co-authors abandoned it. Both had been "lightly committed members," so that wasn't too surprising. On the other hand, five members who had been strongly committed from the very beginning "passed through this period of disconfirmation and its aftermath with their faith firm, unshaken, and lasting." Two others, who had gone through an earlier period of doubt, "emerged from the disconfirmation of December 21 [the date set as "the end of the world"] more strongly convinced than before." Those who had started out doubting "reacted to disconfirmation by persisting in their doubts and admitting their disillusionment and confusion, but still not completely disavowing" the prophesies of the group's founder. This last group had passed through some period of isolation from the group, which Festinger and his co-editors indicated might have had some effect on their reaction to the disconfirmation.[119]

While many on the left will find the comparison of our situation to that of a cult not only inappropriate but insulting, I believe that with a little humility, we might be able to learn something about human behavior and what might be forthcoming as the Pink Tide recedes and leaves barren stretches of sand and wreckage in its wake.

It is in the nature of life and physical laws, after all, for processes to begin, reach a peak of energy, face entropy and then die, or enter into *enantiodromia*, changing into their opposite. Venezuela is already rapidly approaching its terminal point and in all likelihood will soon become an outright military or civic-military dictatorship or return to a liberal democracy with what Dornbusch and Edwards describe as "Phase 4" of the populist economic cycle, when "Orthodox stabilization [that is, IMF intervention, structural adjustment programs, devaluation, etc.] takes over under a new government."

For North American activists, all this should raise many questions about the issues of anti-imperialism and solidarity. But so far there's been astoundingly little debate in left media, as many people seem to fear voicing doubts about the Venezuelan "revolution" and have great resistance to any critical discussion or debate. One thing that the Venezuelan crisis that started in February 2014 reveals is that a large percent of the US left still has much work ahead to redefine its vision, its views and itself.

When students and their allies in Venezuela took to the streets to express their outrage over shortages, media censorship, violence, impunity and the apparent indifference of the Bolivarian government to the nation's growing problems, North American activists in their great majority sided with the Bolivarian government and blamed the disturbances on "US government interference." Worse still, left media outlets mounted attacks on Human Rights Watch and other human rights organizations as well as others critical of the government's handling of the uprising.[120] My own attempts to publish the Venezuelan student and

104

social movement organizations' perspectives were met with silence, or hostility. Across the board discussion was refused, dissent silenced, and all alternative perspectives rejected out-of-hand in support of what was effectively the Bolivarian party line, while left solidarity activists descended to personal attacks and censorship in response to dissenting viewpoints.

Tragically, in keeping with Festinger et al.'s study, it seems that we can expect even more of that as disconfirmation increases. It seems probable that a majority on the "old" left will more vociferously defend the Bolivarians and their policies, while continuing to blame the problems on "imperialism" or the "economic sabotage" of the capitalist class—both real issues, but not the central causes of the problems in Venezuela today.[121] Unless people on the US left choose to let go of entrenched biases and engage in dialogue, they will most likely continue to shut out all dissonant information not in harmony with their current views, and become increasingly more bewildered and confused by events that continue to disconfirm their beliefs.

It will require great courage and humility to confront and resolve the questions raised by Venezuela and the other governments of the Pink Tide. The answers may not fit comfortably into the dogmas and safe positions of the past; we'll have to learn to define a new set of principles and stake out new territory against elite state power blocks of the "right" and "left," where both follow the dictates of the Transnational Capitalist State (TNS). We'll have to choose to define new spaces with new ideas or we'll be left defending old, worn-out, dysfunctional dogmas against the same on the other side.

While it's clear that our anti-imperialist stance will remain positioned against our government in defense of governments throughout Latin America, especially those of the Pink Tide, and while we acknowledge the dangers those governments face from their own internal contradictions, we have yet to determine where we need to place our solidarity, and how.

Anti-imperialism is a position one takes against an empire-building government and in favor of its target. It doesn't necessarily imply "solidarity," even if the two words were conflated in the twentieth century when vanguard parties took state power with the support of a majority of the people. But even then, more critical activists were able to distinguish between a protective anti-imperialist stance toward a government targeted by imperialist forces, and solidarity with that nation's people.

The word "solidarity" arose in the struggles of the 19th century from the word "solidary" which means "solid-like." While a stance or position evokes the image of a line of people facing off against an army or a police battalion or other force representing the state, solidarity brings to mind the other side of that imagined struggle, a standing *with people*. We've seen and experienced such "solidarity" over the past decades in our own country when protesters of all races, class backgrounds, ages and interests have linked arms to create a solid block. That remains for me the image of solidarity, and as well, in the solidarity movement cited earlier in this book.

I have a difficult time understanding how anyone who defines him or herself as "left" could link arms with a soldier or policeman or any representative of any state no matter how benign or

106

"progressive," when that state is undertaking actions against a civilian population. And I also have a difficult time grasping how anyone could justify armed attacks by police, military or paramilitaries of any government against demonstrators who are, for the most part, unarmed, as the Bolivarian government did in the spring of 2014.

There may be valid reasons for withdrawing support or maintaining a critical distance from a social movement's activities. In fact, there are good reasons to *always* maintain a critical consciousness when acting in concert and solidarity with social movements. Healthy movements thrive on the critical consciousness of their members. Yet each time we consider extending solidarity to any group we consider to be a force for social transformation, especially as we recognize the incapacity of governments—be they of the left or the right—we need to look to the people themselves.

More importantly, as we consider the work of solidarity, we need to look more closely at ourselves. Are we clinging to a hope for change in the face of "disconfirmation" of facts and realities that indicate a contrary direction to the one we hope for? Do we continue to believe our salvation comes from the heroics of leaders who are in reality hungry to hold on to power, or do we really understand that "only the people can save the people"?

This is not to take an ideologically anarchist stance and refuse all governments. Rather, my goal is to clarify that alliances of movements with governments should be strategically considered and critically undertaken, while always protecting the movement's autonomy. Humberto Cholango was quite clear about this when he talked about ECUARUNARI's strategy:

> it consists of social mobilization, obviously, but we also need a strategy not only of protest, but also of proposals and alternatives... We can't say [President Rafael] Correa is our friend, nor even our enemy: he's heading a government of transition with dramatic effects, but not under a [social] project. So it will depend a lot on the power, the consciousness of social forces, whether or not they'll allow Correa to continue on this path or, if not, whether they'll force him, by a mobilization of the people, to work in their interest.[122]

Above all, we can't expect governments to build any of those mechanisms of liberation for us. They haven't the will, and even if they did, they lack the ability, given the nature of the TNS that rules them. Their room for movement is minimal to non-existent so severely are they restricted by the international mechanisms of the IMF, the GATT and other structures of the TNS that dominate the global economy. The TNS exerts enormous pressure and governments respond. But they also respond to pressure from organized people, if, indeed, those people apply pressure.

Humberto Cholango knew well about power and working from within the system to transform it. He had been part of organizations that supported, and then were betrayed by, President Lucio Gutierrez. Cholango tells about how taking spaces in the government only means "you're administering those spaces. You have a heavy bureaucracy, a clumsy bureaucracy, the mentality of which is formed in neoliberalism... you have no power because you're a minister or director or something else" and occupying that position meant that one was "used, in that post, used by [the bureaucracy's] neoliberal interests."[123]

Oscar Olivera, a social movement organizer in Bolivia, is even more explicit, saying that, "It is not a struggle between parties or leaders" but between the people in movement and the TNS. Referring back to the TIPNIS struggle, he asks who defines economic policies around the world, answers that, "It's the bankers, the transnationals. And here, who defines where the highway goes through the TIPNIS? Evo Morales? The government? No, it's the Brazilian transnationals who are interested in having a route for exporting iron to China. So the states have left off being states as such."[124]

It's crucial to recognize, and therefore bears repeating, that movements under Pink Tide governments are facing the same challenges and threats from their governments as movements in countries of the region with right wing governments. Their situations are not distinct. Stuart Kirsch is quite clear on this point when he writes that,

> ...policies toward extractive industry by left of centre governments claiming to represent the interests of the people, such as the social movement state of Evo Morales in Bolivia and Rafael Correa's post-neoliberal state in Ecuador, do not differ significantly from the policies of their predecessors, or even from the policies of Alan García's conservative neoliberal state in Peru. For the state to learn from social movements, it

must be willing to acknowledge the legitimacy of their concerns, or at the very least be willing to establish some kind of pragmatic detente. However, the case studies suggest that states are often reluctant to compromise with their critics. Instead, Morales and Correa both aggressively dismiss their complaints, with Morales justifying his actions by claiming to act on behalf of the "common good," whereas Correa exploits his popularity to intimidate critics of mining.[125]

The solution remains with us. It's only by "building resistance to power" by means of autonomous, critical, often oppositional, movements, that we'll move forward. Again, Cholango: "So this resistance and building of [our] power is essential, but so is globalizing this struggle and weaving alliances." As North American activists we have to begin to find a way to do anti-imperialist solidarity in two steps: Opposing our government by taking a protective stance in regard to target governments at the same time that we offer our solidarity to the people in their struggle under those target governments. It won't be a simple procedure and we may risk alienating allies and strengthening enemies in the process. But it will get easier with practice, reflection, and still more practice. It's an approach many in the radical Christian peace and anti-imperialist movements have long been familiar with.

Solidarity is just as much about reaching into the great world beyond our borders to offer our presence there as it is to bring the presence of the great world beyond back into our communities. We might consider in this context the Buddhist view that salvation comes in two forms. One, known as "the lesser vehicle" of Hinayana, consists in cultivating one's own holiness, spirituality and progress through ethical conduct in one's own life. This is admirable, but it isn't comparable to "Mahayana" or "the great-vehicle," in which one's salvation comes through actions aimed at rescuing others from the corruption of the world.

In a similar way, as we intensify our struggle against capitalist extraction and destruction of the environment for monetary "profit," we can choose two courses. We can become either "localists," focusing on our *own* communities and lives: building community gardens, developing community cohesion through projects with our neighbors, reducing, reusing and recycling, putting solar on our roofs, driving less and bicycling more, supporting organic food production, and a host of other things that can not only improve our lives and health, or we can do all of the above while also offering a model to our community of a new and healthier way to live. This is "Hinayana" and it's good and admirable. But in our time, I would argue, we should not stop there. We need to move on with "Mahayana" and extend this vision of life beyond our own community and into the larger world.

Transnational organizing to build larger structures of solidarity can facilitate cross-border solidarity actions between workers of different countries. Much of this is being done and it complements the work of organizing low-wage workers in the United States and other local labor struggles. The climate justice movement displays this same transnational solidarity and international awareness. The Boycott Divestment and Sanctions campaign is yet another great example of a "counter-hegemonic project led by popular classes" that would "move 'up' cross-nationally." The list of work already being done with this focus is long and inspiring. We just need to strengthen that work and open our minds to the possibilities for building solidarity at home and abroad, people-to-people, as we enter into the work of making viable the "Great Vehicle" that might take us to that other, possible world.

Where does that leave us? I hope this awareness that the old "answers" no longer serve us humbles us and makes us willing to let those old ideas go. I hope the pain of "disconfirmation" drives us to abandon those old ideas entirely. I hope our sense of hopelessness will not end there in a state of helpless cynicism. I hope it will inspire us to begin to look for new solutions, solutions that remain invisible to us as long as we cling to the old, broken, dysfunctional and outdated "solutions." I hope we will gather in our local communities with our friends and allies and welcome in our former enemies, should they wish to join us, so that together we can find a path forward in this great darkness that envelops us in the present moment. I hope that in that community, with differences and unity of purpose at our core, we can encounter the strength of what the original peoples all over the world, our own ancestors, knew as the "Great Spirit" and that we might look to this Power we don't understand to light our way.

I am no longer a religious person, but I do believe we have to embark on a new quest for spiritual values that will allow us to appreciate life over death, people and all living creatures over the illusion of money, and to abandon materialist and materialistic views of development so we might truly develop as humans: heart, mind, soul, spirit and body.

I often reflect on the story of Moses and the Golden Calf for its profound symbolic significance, and I think it reveals a way out of our present tangle as we search for solutions to the deadly forces that threaten our lives and our planet. In the story, Moses returns from his time in communion with God to find that the people of Israel had stripped themselves of the gold that epitomized their beauty, splendor and glory, and thrown it together to create a calf which they now worshipped. Moses' saw their social disempowerment and blind, stupid idolatry of an externalized power, and his response was simple and brilliant. We read in Exodus that, "he took the calf which they had made and burnt it with fire and ground it to powder, and scattered it upon the water, and made the people of Israel drink it."[126]

And so the people, who looked to idols of power to save them, in the end were forced to take the beauty that once outwardly adorned them back into themselves, where it belonged. And then they were ready to enter the Promised Land – or better, perhaps, the "Possible Land."

End Notes

[1] http://www.directionsmag.com/features/a-more-realistic-view-of-our-world/129763

[2] *Venezuela: Revolution from the Inside Out* (Oakland: PM Press, 2008)

[3] My articles from this time can be found at our website, www.latinamericansocialmovements.org a

[4] http://bigstory.ap.org/article/venezuela-opposition-wants-probe-violence

[5] For a delightful discussion of the long history of money, see Jack Weatherford, *The History of Money* (New York: Crown Publishers, 1997)

[6] David Hawkes, *Ideology*, Second Edition (New York: Routledge, 2003) p. 6

[7] Georg Simmel, *The Philosophy of Money* (New York: Routledge, 2004) p. 223. Also quoted in Weatherford, *The History of Money*.

[8] William Robinson, *Latin America and Global Capitalism: A Critical Globalization Perspective* (Baltimore: Johns Hopkins University Press, 2008) p.38

[9] Richard Seymour, *American Insurgents: A Brief History of American Anti-Imperialism* (Chicago: Haymarket Books, 2012). Much of the history recounted here is drawn from this book, except where otherwise noted.

[10] See Walter LaFeber's interview at http://www.pbs.org/wgbh/amex/1900/filmmore/reference/interview/lafeber_antiimperialism.html

[11] Seymour, *American Insurgents*, p. 200

[12] Many of the remarkable documents have been archived at http://www.antiimperialist.com/documents/leaguepublications/84-american-leaguedocs

[13] ibid.

[14] ibid; also see : http://www.fordham.edu/halsall/mod/1899antiimp.asp

[15] Seymour, p. 50

[16] See Alan McPherson, *The Invaded* (Oxford University Press, 2014) p. 221

[17] Seymour, *American Insurgents*, p. 72

[18] This is the recollection of my "elder," more reliable comrades who were deeply involved in the movement during those years.

[19] Seymour, for instance, doesn't offer so much as a footnote in his book to the Quakers, Catholic Workers or the historic "Peace Churches."

[20] "Historical Determinants of the Latin American State: The Tradition of Bureaucratic-Patrimonialism, Corporatism, Centralism, and Authoritarianism" by Howard J. Wiarda in Howard J. Wiarda and Margaret Macleish Mott, *Politics and Social Change in Latin America: Still a Distinct Tradition?* Fourth Edition (Westport, CT: Praeger, 2003) p. 140

[21] Leo Panitch and Sam Gindin, *The Making of Global Capitalism* (New York: Verso, 2012) p. 104

[22] Panitch and Gindin, p. 105

[23] Among the many works on this period and the role of the U.S. on recent work stands out: Greg Grandin, *The Empire's Workshop* (New York: Henry Holt, 2007)

[24] David Harvey, *A Brief History of Neoliberalism* (New York: Oxford University Press, 2007) p. 29

[25] Panitch and Gindin, p. 214

[26] Panitch and Gindin, p.215

[27] See Robinson, op cit.

[28] http://www.reuters.com/article/2013/05/27/venezuela-chevron-idUSL2N0E80OM20130527 see also http://www.theglobeandmail.com/report-on-business/international-business/latin-american-business/china-to-loan-4-billion-to-venezuela-in-exchange-for-oil/article19699329/

[29] http://www.huffingtonpost.com/2013/05/31/ecuador-oil-spill-sote-pipeline_n_3368520.html

[30] http://humboldt.org.ni/blog/2014/01/31/estado-actual-del-sector-minero-y-sus-impactos-socioambientales-en-nicaragua

[31] Anthony Bebbington, "Extractive Industries, socio-environmental conflicts and political economic

transformations in Andean America" in Anthony Bebbington, editor, *Social Conflict, Economic Development and Extractive Industry: Evidence from South America* (New York: Routledge, 2013) p. 6

[32] Rafael Uzcátegui, Revolution as Spectacle (Tucson: See Sharp Press, 2010) p. 153

[33] Charles Tilly and Lesley J. Wood, *Social Movements: 1768-2008* Second Edition (Boulder: Paradigm Publishers, 2009) p. 54

[34] Clifton Ross and Marcy Rein, *Until the Rulers Obey: Voices from Latin American Social Movements* (Oakland: PM Press, 2014) p. 321

[35] http://www.yachana.org/research/lapleft.pdf

[36] http://amazonwatch.org/work/belo-monte-dam

[37] Marina Sitrin and Dario Azzellini, *They Can't Represent Us! Reinventing Democracy from Greece to Occupy* (Brooklyn: Verso, 2014) p. 212

[38] The story is compelling reading, but it has unfortunately since been taken down from the website at http://www.theguardian.com/lifeandstyle/2010/jan/10/malcolm-caldwell-pol-pot-murder

[39] Roger Burbach, Michael Fox and Federico Fuentes, *Latin America's Turbulent Transitions* (New York: Zed Books, 2013). See our review, "The New Socialism," *NACLA Report on the Americas* , Vol. 46, No. 2

[40] Anabella Abadi M. "15 años de Revolución Bolivariana en cifras," Monday, December 16th, 2013 at www.prodavinci.com

[41] Archived at http://venezuelandailybrief.blogspot.com/2014/04/april-08-2014.html

[42] http://www.eluniversal.com/nacional-y-politica/140712/targeting-productive-lands

[43] These are issues dealt with in the final third of my feature film, *Venezuela: Revolution from the Inside Out* (Oakland: PM Press, 2008). Since the making of that film, I have become far more critical of the Bolivarian Revolution.

[44] Prat's research is summed up in an excellent analysis that can be found online in Spanish at

http://gumilla.org/biblioteca/bases/biblo/texto/SIC20117 32_62-65.pdf

[45] Ross and Rein, p. 206

[46] Ibid, p. 205

[47] Rafael Uzcátegui, op. cit. in Spanish, my translation. Also found in the English edition cited above, p. 138

[48] Javier Corrales and Michael Penfold, *Dragon in the Tropics: Hugo Chávez and the Political Economy of Revolution in Venezuela* (Washington DC: Brookings Institution, 2011) p. 138

[49] http://www.telesurtv.net/english/news/Maduro-Announces-Five-Big-Revolutions-in-Venezuela-20140902-0053.html

[50] Terry Karl, *The Paradox of Plenty: Oil Booms and Petro-States* (Berkeley: University of California Press, 1997) p. 16

[51] Margarita López Maya, "Hugo Chávez and the Populist Left" in Steven Levitsky and Kenneth Roberts, *The Resurgence of the Latin American Left* (Baltimore: The Johns Hopkins University Press, 2011) p. 214

[52] Corrales and Penfold, p. 9

[53] http://online.wsj.com/news/articles/SB1000142405270 2303874504579377542520825148

[54] http://uk.reuters.com/article/2014/07/02/uk-venezuela-plot-idUKKBN0F72GT20140702

[55] http://www.csmonitor.com/World/Americas/Latin-America-Monitor/2011/0830/Is-29-billion-missing-from-Hugo-Chávez-s-Fonden-development-fund

[56] http://www.reuters.com/article/2013/12/12/us-venezuela-economy-idUSBRE9BB0T820131212

[57] http://caracaschronicles.com/2014/08/26/things-you-find-in-your-septic-tank/

[58] The discussion distinguishing between "socialism" and "state capitalism" was particularly passionate in the mid-twentieth century. The Johnson-Forest Tendency, a Trotskyist schism which included C.L.R. James, Grace Lee Boggs and others made a convincing case that the Soviet Union was a "state capitalist" enterprise. Their argument is developed, in the heavy, clunky language of the day, thanks to a PM Press reprint, C.L.R. James, *State*

117

Capitalism and World Revolution (Oakland: PM Press, 2013).
[59] David Hawkes, *Ideology* (New York, Routledge, 1996), p. 16-17
[60]

http://www.eluniversal.com/economia/130218/calculan-que-274-de-las-importaciones-fueron-ficticias
[61] http://www.eluniversal.com/economia/140529/en-10-anos-las-importaciones-ficticias-fueron-69-millardos
[62] http://www.eluniversal.com/nacional-y-politica/130524/transcript-of-mario-silvas-recording
[63]

http://transitions.foreignpolicy.com/posts/2014/01/30/fair_profits_in_venezuela
[64]http://www.bbc.co.uk/mundo/noticias/2012/01/111207_venezuela_economia_expropiaciones_chavez_jp.shtml
[65] http://www.manosfueradevenezuela.org/24-noticias/noticias/408-venezuela-nacionaliza-la-industria-cementera.html
[66] http://publicoyconfidencial.com/esos-mismos-98-que-negaron-investigar-pudreval-mafia-de-las-cabillas-cartel-del-hierro-bandes/
[67] http://publicoyconfidencial.com/pc-a-ver-sr-maduro-explique-por-que-cuesta-tanto-conseguir-cabillas-y-cemento-si-el-gobierno-es-dueno-de-todo/
[68] I go into these issues in greater depth in articles I've published different places on the web, and now archived at www.latinamericansocialmovements.org.
[69] http://publicoyconfidencial.com/pc-la-revolucion-del-70-menos-y-mas-ruina/
[70] http://www.eluniversal.com/economia/130821/unete-asegura-que-gestion-gubernamental-ha-colapsado-a-empresas-estati
[71] Corrales and Penfold, p. 62
[72] Rudiger Dornbusch and Sebastian Edwards, *The Macroeconomics of Populism in Latin America* (Chicago: University of Chicago Press, 1991) pp. 11-12
[73] Javier Corrales, "Conflicting Goals in Venezuela's Foreign Policy" in Ralph S. Clem and Anthony P.

Maingot, eds, Venezuela's Petro-Diplomacy: Hugo
Chávez's Foreign Policy (Gainesville: University Press of
Florida, 2011) p. 33

[74] David González, *El Estado Descomunal:
Conversaciones con Margarita Lopez Maya* (Caracas,
Venezuela: Editorial CEC, SA, Los Libros de El Nacional,
2013) p. 55

[75] Casto Ocando, *Chavistas en el Imperio: Secretos,
Tácticas, y Escándalos de la Revolución Boivariana en
los Estados Unidos* (Miami: Factual Editores, 2014) p. 10

[76] Katherine Vega, quoting Manuel Malaver in
"Devaluación pone al riesgo la revolución," El
Comercio, April 16, 2013

[77]http://prodavinci.com/2014/08/26/actualidad/deuda-
del-gobierno-con-el-sector-industrial-esta-entre-7-y-9-
millardos-de-us-monitorprodavinci/

[78] Carlos de la Torre, *Populist Seduction in Latin
America*, Second Edition (Ohio: Center for International
Studies, 2010) Preface ix

[79] Carlos de la Torre, 2010, p. viii

[80] Kurt Weyland, "The Performance of Leftist
Governments in Latin America," in Kurt Weyland, Raúl
L. Madrid, Wendy Hunder, eds. *Leftist Governments in
Latin America: Successes and Shortcomings* (New York:
Cambridge University Press, 2010) p. 16

[81] ibid

[82] Allan R. Brewer-Carías, *Dismantling Democracy in
Venezuela: The Chávez Authoritarian Experiment* (New
York: Cambridge University Press, 2010) p. 13

[83] Brewer-Carías, op. cit.

[84] VenEconomía Opina, August 29, 2014

[85] http://en.wikipedia.org/wiki/Antonio_Ledezma

[86]http://www.globalpost.com/dispatch/news/regions/ame
ricas/venezuela/110811/Politics-Venezuela-Oppression-
Chavez

[87] ibid.

[88] Carlos de la Torre, 2010, p. 151

[89] David González, Op. cit.

[90] ibid.

[91] See Rafael Uzcátegui, Op. cit.

[92] Ross and Rein, pp. 191-201
[93] Cristina Marcano and Alberto Barrera Tyszka, Hugo Chávez: *The Definitive Biography of Venezuela's Controversial President* (New York: Random House, 2007) p. 268
[94] Marcano and Tyszka, p. 269
[95] Marcano and Tyszka, p. 270
[96]See my article at http://www.counterpunch.org/2013/07/19/building-a-critical-left-solidarity-movement/, also archived at www.latinamericansocialmovements.org
[97]

http://www.elmundo.com.ve/noticias/economia/politicas-publicas/el-costo-de-la-vida-aumento-74-8--en-un-ano--segun.aspx#ixzz34plnrf9d
[98] According to Datanalisis, see http://www.eluniversal.com/economia/140415/escasez-de-alimentos-basicos-se-ubico-en-602-en-marzo
[99] http://prodavinci.com/2014/08/28/actualidad/dr-jackson-ochoa-vocero-de-la-avch-nunca-habia-visto-una-situacion-como-la-que-vivimos/
[100] See http://en.wikipedia.org/wiki/Detention_of_Maria_Lourdes_Afiuni
[101] See http://en.wikipedia.org/wiki/Ra%C3%BAl_Baduel
[102]

http://www.eluniversal.com/economia/140424/tribunal-declara-inocente-a-sindicalista-ruben-gonzalez
[103] Ross and Rein, pp. 201-204
[104]http://www.worldbank.org/en/country/venezuela/overview
[105]Political discrimination is detailed in this early report from Human Rights Watch: http://www.hrw.org/reports/2008/venezuela0908/2.htm
[106] Programa Venezolana de Educación-Acción en Derechos Humanos (Provea) Edición Nro.10 Febrero 2014 page 3
[107]Matthew Yeomans, *Oil: Anatomy of an Industry* (New York: New Press, 2004) p. 111

[108] http://uk.reuters.com/article/2014/08/27/oil-venezuela-imports-idUKL1N0QX1JJ20140827
[109] http://www.forbes.com/sites/christopherhelman/2014/02/20/cheap-gasoline-why-venezuela-is-doomed-to-collapse/
[110] See Ross and Rein, p. 184
[111] See Committee to Protect Journalism's special report by Monica Campbell at http://www.cpj.org/reports/2012/08/after-years-of-assault-venezuelas-independent-pres.php
[112] http://www.csmonitor.com/World/Americas/Latin-America-Monitor/2014/0509/Venezuela-Polls-show-Maduro-approval-dropping-after-3-months-of-protest . That is, unless one considers that by August, 2014 after six months of protest, "only" 54% of Venezuelans believe he should resign or be turned out of office in a 2016 referendum. See http://puzkas.com/evaluacion-del-gobierno-es-la-peor-en-una-decada/
[113] Daniel Hellinger, *Venezuela: Tarnished Democracy* (Boulder: Westview Press, 1991) p. 198
[114] http://prodavinci.com/2014/08/16/actualidad/julio-coco-y-marea-socialista-rebelion-en-las-bases-del-chavismo-y-la-oposicion-por-franz-von-bergen/
[115] http://www.project-syndicate.org/commentary/roberto-laserna-cautions-against-excessive-confidence-in-the-region-s-capacity-for-sustained-economic-reform
[116] Weyland, Madrid, Hunter, p. 11
[117] Weyland, Madrid, Hunter, p. 13
[118] Leon Festinger, Henry W. Riecken and Stanley Schachter, *When Prophesy Fails* (Minneapolis: University of Minnesota, 1956) p. 26
[119] Festinger et al., p. 208
[120] The most distressing example was allowing the pillorying of Human Rights Watch for their presumed bias on Venezuela on the June 11, 2014 *Democracy Now* show, even though Amy Goodman seems to consider the organization a reliable enough source on virtually every other issue and country.

[121] The topic of "economic sabotage" is enormous and too complicated to address here at any length. For Spanish readers I recommend Prat's book, Guayana: El Milagro al Reves. This brief blog post also breaks down the argument well: http://www.washingtonpost.com/blogs/wonkblog/wp/2014/08/29/why-are-venezuelas-supermarkets-so-empty/ and there are many good articles archived at www.caracaschronicles.com. For those who want to keep up with intelligent and informed information about Venezuela, this latter website is indispensable.
[122] Ross and Rein, p. 222-223
[123] Ross and Rein, pp. 224-225
[124] Ross and Rein, p. 327
[125] Stuart Kirsch, "Afterword: Extractive conflicts compared" in Anthony Bebbington, p. 201
[126] Exodus 32:20, *Bible* (Revised Standard Version).